Author's Note

Warren Buffett is commonly known as a longterm investor. But, if you have a look at the list of companies where Berkshire Hathaway, the company owned by Warren Buffett, has stakes, you would be surprised to find that it has 90% to 100% holdings in 67 other companies. These subsidiary companies are in major or controlling positions in different consumer markets and together they earn revenue of USD 109 billion (2017). Besides this, Berkshire Hathaway also has stakes ranging from 0.01% to 27.25% in 42 other companies. With all this, Berkshire Hathaway was making a net profit of USD 24.07 billion (2016) out of the total revenue of USD 223.60 billion. This also is a testimony to Warren Buffett's great management acumen.

And in both of these forms, the core mantra of Warren Buffett's success has been—picking the right business. Yes, long before starting his professional life as an investor, Buffett had already uncovered the mystery that all the businesses did not have the same economics, and there were some specific kinds of businesses whose economics by nature worked profusely in their favour. He had deciphered that the companies that got support from their inherent economics required minimal capital investment as compared to their earnings. These kind of companies mostly manufactured brand products that never needed to be replaced. Or else, they provided such vital services that did not have any competitive substitute. Thus, they are in a way 'monopoly businesses' only. Hence, these companies had the freedom to charge more for their products and services, thus providing them much better profit margins.

That is the reason that, during his entire professional life, Warren Buffett has always been looking for such specific businesses that enjoyed support from their inherent economics and he has been considering them only the 'right businesses'. Evidently, picking the 'right business' has been the most important aspect of Warren Buffett's investment strategy. However, Warren Buffett's main objective has not been only to make a regular income by picking the 'right business' and investing in the same; instead, he wants to even acquire ownership of the 'right business'. Not only that, he also wants to work for the 'right business' in order to help the same in attaining its optimum potentials. But he is not interested in only making maximum profits by exploiting the optimum potentials of the 'right business'; rather he wants to maintain his holding in that company as long as possible, as he believes that a 'right business' also provides greatest career opportunities.

Thus, Warren Buffett is of the opinion that only those companies that are in a position to provide career advancement, job security and greatest opportunities for sustainable earnings can be the most suitable for ownership, investment and to work with. Warren Buffett considers such companies only as the 'right businesses' capable of providing 'durable competitive advantage', as their inherent economics work in their favour. But, the matter does not end here. Warren Buffett further subjects these 'right businesses' to serious financial analysis, techniques of which would be presented to you in detail in the second chapter.

However, for Warren Buffett, it is not enough to just pick the 'right business' and perform its 'financial analysis'; he pays equal attention to choose the 'right manager' for running that business. Just think, Warren Buffett had taken over control of Berkshire Hathaway almost 53 years back in May 1965. During that period, the market value of its shares kept growing at the rate of 21% pa whereas the average annual return of Dow Jones Industrial Average (DJAI) was only 2.075%. Now, the question

MONEY MAKING SKILLS BY WARREN BUFFETT

PRADEEP THAKUR

PRABHAT PRAKASHAN

Published by
PRABHAT PRAKASHAN PVT. LTD.
4/19 Asaf Ali Road,
New Delhi-110 002 (INDIA)
e-mail: prabhatbooks@gmail.com

ISBN 978-93-5562-659-2
MONEY MAKING SKILLS BY WARREN BUFFETT
by Pradeep Thakur

Edition
2026

Price
₹ 300 (Rupees Three Hundred Only)

Printed at
Yash Printographics, Noida

comes up naturally - how was it possible for Warren Buffett to achieve such an amazing performance? Most of the people would just say that he is the greatest investor of the world. Of course, there is not an iota of doubt in the fact that Warren Buffett has been the greatest and the most successful investor of our time. But, this is not a full answer to the question. In fact, the most important point to understand in respect of Warren Buffett is that he has been an exceptionally successful 'manager' also.

Yes, Warren Buffett is that single particular individual who has been in control of the huge multinational conglomerate like Berkshire Hathaway continuously for the last 53 years. However, even most of the followers of Warren Buffett's investment strategy have not made serious attempts to understand and absorb his 'management sutras'. Had that happened, multinational corporates would have definitely undergone transformation in their work culture. You are going to read in the third chapter, how Warren Buffett had gone ahead with his selection of the 'right managers' for his different businesses and how he had developed for himself the art of delegation of authority to those 'right managers'. But, Warren Buffett had gone ahead still further and had also developed the unique art of motivating the managers; you will read about the same in fourth chapter. This was the reason that Warren Buffett had transformed various businesses of Berkshire Hathaway into a powerful business empire. You would be surprised to know how much Warren Buffett had learnt from other people, including the pioneer of self-development Dale Carnegie and how he had incorporated those lessons into his management style. Be it the skill of making impression in the very first meeting or the magic of showing appreciation or dangers of making criticism or precise use of counselling - Warren Buffett is ranked at the top among the most efficient leaders of the modern age in respect of encouraging, motivating and influencing their managers.

However, as a business expands, its growth providing opportunities for better earnings is also accompanied with problems and challenges. In Warren Buffett's opinion, business pathways are replete with pitfalls and disaster planning is required to safeguard against them. He counts risks associated with excessive credits, violations of rules by employees, straying away from good thoughts, making unintentional mistakes, inability to manage sycophants and missing right opportunities as the pitfalls of business pathways and lays emphasis on using specific management techniques to confront all those problems and challenges. Buffett believes that only when we are capable of managing them, we would be able to notice the opportunities of concerned businesses. However, Buffett had, on the basis on his experiences, gradually developed his disaster planning for safeguarding against those pitfalls. In the fifth and the last chapter, we are going to discuss Buffett's those very invaluable experiences that would help every leader in keeping himself away from those management pitfalls and extricating himself out of them.

I am sure, 'Money Making Skills' would not only provide an opportunity to the sensible readers to understand the 'money skills' of the greatest investor of the world but also help them in ensuring success in their personal and professional life by applying these management sutras.

❑

Contents

1

Picking the Right Business

Warren Buffett has not only been a long-term investor but also an exceptional business manager. And in both of these 'avatars', the core mantra of Warren Buffett's success has been - picking the right business.

Yes, long before starting his professional life as an investor, Buffett had already uncovered the mystery that all the businesses did not have the same economics, and there were some specific kinds of businesses whose economics by nature worked profusely in their favour. The companies with such inherent business economics required minimal capital investment as compared to their earnings. This kind of companies mostly manufactured brand products that never needed to be replaced. Or else, they provided such vital services that did not have any competitive substitute. Thus, they are in a way 'monopoly businesses' only. That is the reason these companies had the freedom to charge more for their products and services, thus providing them much better profit margins.

During his entire professional life, Warren Buffett has always been looking for such specific businesses only that enjoyed favourable inherent business economics, as he considers them only the 'right businesses'. Buffett always believed discovering or picking the 'right business' to be the most important aspect of his investment strategy. However, his main objective has been not only to make a regular income by picking a 'right business' and investing in the same; Warren wants to even acquire ownership of the 'right business'. Not only that, he also wants to work for the 'right business' in order to help the same in attaining its optimum potentials. But, he is not interested in only making maximum profits by exploiting the optimum potentials of the 'right business'; rather he wants to maintain his holding in that company as long as possible, as he believes that a 'right business' also provides greatest career opportunities.

Companies Having Durable Competitive Advantage

Warren Buffett is of the opinion that only those companies that are in a position to provide career advancement, job security and greatest opportunities for sustainable earnings can be the most suitable for ownership, investment and to work with. Warren Buffett considers such companies only as the 'right businesses' capable of providing 'durable competitive advantage', as their inherent business economics work in their favour.

In fact, these companies have basic products and services that are certainly always in demand but they never require too much of modification or alteration. Hence, such companies do not have to make huge investments in upgradation of plant and machinery either for research and development or on account of modifications in product design. These companies continue to run their old plant and machinery for years with minimal maintenance expenses, until they wear away completely. Thus, the companies use such huge saved funds for expansion of their business, and they neither have to go for bank borrowings at high interest rates nor have to raise funds from market by issuing fresh shares of equity. Not only that, it is also generally easy to sell such basic products and services and they are able to keep their brand image set in consumers' minds without incurring too much of advertisement expenses. For these very reasons, such products and services are always in heavy demand that helps concerned companies attain high levels of profit margin associated with high sales volume. In such a case, these companies generate cash internally to the extent that they are able to continuously expand their business out of their own funds.

For example, companies like Coca-Cola do not need to invest billions of dollars on continuous improvement in design or quality of their products and upgradation of their plant and machinery for the same to maintain their competitive edge. Thus, such companies accumulate enough cash to make them capable of taking over other companies to expand their market without resorting to borrowings or selling their shares of equity. On the other hand, take a look at the companies like General Motors. The designs of their products - automobiles, keep changing almost every year and they have to spend billions of dollars every year on upgradation of their plant and machinery. If General Motors does not do that, it would not be able to compete with companies like Ford Motors and Toyota. This is the reason that, for meeting their capital expenditure requirements, all the companies in automobile industry have to resort to sale of bonds and shares of equity along with bank borrowings over and above their sales revenue.

Since, in this case, the 'inherent business economics' of the soft drink industry works in favour of companies like Coca-Cola, they are able to provide durable competitive advantage. On the other hand, the 'inherent business economics' of the automobile industry does not work in favour of companies like General Motors and they are not capable of providing durable competitive advantage. Now the question arises as to which of the two kinds of companies can provide career development, job security and the best opportunities for long-term earnings - one that is capable of generating huge amount of cash internally, or the other that is burning huge amounts of cash? We all would have the same answer - the companies that are generating huge amounts of cash, as extra cash holdings reflect well on the management of those companies and also provide them generous bonus at the end of every year. It is obvious that such companies only can provide job security to their employees and also opportunities to their shareholders for better earnings.

It is clear that Warren considers only such companies the 'right companies' that are capable of providing durable and competitive advantage. Such companies have three basic business models - those who sell unique products, those who provide unique services and those who trade in low-cost products and services that are part of common people's needs and are always in heavy demand.

Companies Selling Unique Products

We may include Coca-Cola Company, PepsiCo Inc., Philip Morris Marlboro, Budweiser (Anheuser-Busch InBev Group), Gillette (Proctor & Gamble/ P & G), Hershey Company, Wrigley (Mars, Inc.), Kraft Foods Group, Marc & Co. and Johnson& Johnson etc. among the companies selling unique products. Here, we are providing brief details for unique products of some companies and their brand image.

Coca-Cola Company: Coca-Cola is considered to be the most successful brand of its kind. Everybody has heard the name 'Coca-Cola' and it would be difficult to find a person who would not recognise its red trademark. 'Forbes' magazine had estimated the brand value of 'Coca-Cola' at USD 58.5 billion with 4% annual growth and had placed it at the fourth position among the top 100 most valuable brands of the world in 2016. During that period, 'Coca-Cola' brand alone had earned revenue of USD 21.9 billion whereas Coca-Cola Company had spent only USD 4 billion to promote its brands including 'Coca-Cola'.

Coca-Cola Company is the most significant player among those operating in the non-alcoholic industry across the world. Coca-Cola has its headquarters located at Atlanta, the capital of the state of Georgia in southeast America. This controls and operates the vast network of around 300 bottling plant operators spread across the world through its regional sub-headquarters. During the year 2014, the Company had achieved operating revenue of USD 46 billion which included 46.7% share of North America and that was the biggest market for Coca-Cola. Coca-Cola has a share of around 30% in the world market.

You may be surprised to know that Coca-Cola was not the first to launch a coca-based drink. Coca plants have been grown as a cash crop especially in Argentina, Bolivia, Colombia, Ecuador and Peru in western South America. Coca leaves are known around the world as a source of psychoactive alkaloid 'cocaine', though cocaine content in the same ranges from 0.25% to 0.77% only. Hence, chewing coca leaves or drinking coca tea does not induce feeling of excitement or depression like that caused by cocaine. The juice of coca leaves is being used as medicine for ages; however, it was in 1863 when French chemist Mariani discovered the chemical formula of coca wine. This wine launched in the market with brand name 'Vin Mariani' had become quite popular among the nobility. Nevertheless, the maximum cocaine content in this wine was just 10 mg per ounce and hence, this was very tasty but this induced addiction to drinking.

Twenty-three years after that incident, when 'Vin Mariani' was at the top of its sales in Europe, pharmacist John Pemberton, a retired Lieutenant Colonel of American Army from Georgia, was busy with his experiments to find an alternative for the same. He had created a new wine named 'Pemberton's French Wine Coca' by mixing Coca fruit (a tree native to tropical rainforests of Africa) and damiana leaves (a shrub native to western Texas) with Coca leaves. However, around the same time, the local administration had banned all kinds of alcoholic beverages because of the temperance movement. John Pemberton had then, in 1896, developed a sweet cold drink by modifying the chemical formula of that wine and using seven natural tasty syrups including carbon-based sugar drink, coca leaves and kola fruits. This chemical formula is even today preserved as a secret. Though this was a non-alcoholic drink, it basically had content of cocaine and was launched in the market as a brain tonic. It was not Pemberton but his bookkeeper Frank Robinson who had inspired him to give it the name 'Coca-Cola'. Robinson had used his cursive writing to create the trademark for 'Coca-Cola' that is the most recognised handwriting in the world. Though the credit for suggesting the name goes to Robinson, the honour of Coca-Cola's initial success and popularity is given to Pemberton only.

As such, Pemberton had found it difficult to recover even the production cost for Coca-Cola for the first year. He had started selling Coca-Cola from a medicine shop in Atlanta as a soda fountain drink for five cents a glass. Though the original Coca-Cola also had addiction-inducing properties, it did not prove to be as popular as 'Vin Mariani' and its average daily sale during initial days was limited to just six glasses. However, John Pemberton had proved to be more prudent with respect topromoting and publicising his brand much faster as compared to Angelo Mariani. He had very quickly recognised the power of advertising and had published the first advertisement for Coca-Cola in the local newspaper 'The Atlanta Journal' just three weeks after the drink was invented. This was the reason that while the once popular wine 'Vin Mariani' disappeared from the market due to lack of promotion and publicity, sales of Coca-Cola saw huge jump on the back of advertisements. John Pemberton himself managed advertisements for two years. However, just a week before his death, he sold his interest in Coca-Cola to a local pharmacist and his business friend Asa Griggs Candler.

Candler founded the Coca-Cola Company in 1892 and registered its trademark a year later. However, much before that, in 1885 itself, Candler had executed his expansion plans in all the states of the United Statesand sale of bottled Coca-Cola had started in all major markets. Bottling plants had taken shape during initial years of the 20th century and in the next 100 years, Coca-Cola had established itself as the most recognised brand in the world. It may be noted that the name of 'cocaine' had been already removed from Coca-Cola much earlier and in 1893 itself, its competitor cold drink company the Pepsi-Cola Company had been launched in New Bern (Craven County), North Carolina, an American state close to Georgia; this was constantly trying to compete with Coca-Cola.

Still, Coca-Cola had gone ahead expanding its market as the most successful brand. Why? Because 'Coca-Cola' had made all possible efforts to sustain the market's trust and belief in itself. Now, just have a look at the catch-phrases used by Coca-Cola in its advertisement campaigns - 'The Great National Temperance Drink' (1906), 'Six Million a Day' (1925), 'The Real Thing' (1942), 'What You Want is Coke' (1952), 'Coke is it!' (1982), 'Always Coca-Cola' (1993), etc.

And, don't you remember the historical tag line 'Thanda Matlab Coca-Cola' of the advertisement campaign of Coca-Cola in 2002 in India, which the company had used to enter the rural markets? This tag line in rural language was written by Prasoon Joshi and delivered in the ad film by cine star Amir Khan. At that time, Prasoon was working as a simple copywriter with multinational advertising company Ogilvy & Mather (Delhi). However, this advertisement went on to become so popular that it had won Prasoon Joshi the opportunity to join competing multinational advertising concern McCann Erickson as Executive Vice President and National Creative Director, leaving his almost 10-year old job. Many ad films were created on this tag line and Coca-Cola was able to make its entry into the rural market across India on the back of this campaign.

Of course, the fact that it has always been able to linger in the mind and brain of customers through its incessant ad campaigns based on convincing tag lines has been the greatest strength of the Coca-Cola brand. In 2014 alone, Coca-Cola had spent a total amount of USD 3.50 billion for only this very brand on different ad campaigns and mass-contact activities across the world. The Company had also spent the same USD 3.50 billion on its second biggest brand 'Sprite'. Thus, the Coca-Cola Company was the one spending the most on advertisements during 2015 among all the 100 most valuable brands.

PepsiCo Inc. - PepsiCo is considered to be a differentiation brand. This is not as successful as Coca-Cola. As such, there is no brand on this earth as successful as Coca-Cola, but this also is a fact that it is the majestic position of 'Coca-Cola' that makes 'Pepsi' special, as Pepsi is the only non-alcoholic drink brand that has been able to retain its identity parallel to 'Coca-Cola' for such a long time. You may clearly differentiate between 'Coca-Cola' and 'Pepsi' and that is the reason it is called a differentiation brand. Definitely, this is the best non-alcoholic beverage brand of the world to remain at the second position so close to its main competitor. Although the brand 'Burger King' is also at the position next to McDonald, the gap between the two is quite significant. Such fiercely and closely competing brands like Pepsi and Coca-Cola are not found in this world.

'Forbes' magazine had estimated the brand value of 'Pepsi' at USD 19.3 billion with annual growth of 3% and had placed the same at the 29th position among the 'World's Most Valuable Brands' of 2016. During that period, the Pepsi brand alone had attained a revenue of USD 11.8 billion (USD 39.10 billion less than that of Coca-Cola) whereas PepsiCo had spent USD 2.4 billion on promotion and publicity of all its brands including 'Pepsi'. Thus, by spending just USD 16 million more on advertisement as compared to PepsiCo, the Coca-Cola Company had managed to earn extra revenue of USD 39.10 billion on its primary brand. The Coca-Cola Company had spent 6.8% of its brand revenue on advertisements whereas, PepsiCo had to spend 12.6%. Of course, there is no non-alcoholic beverage brand in between Coca-Cola and Pepsi.

It was in 1893 when University of Maryland School of Medicine educated pharmacist Caleb Davis Bradham had started selling the cold drink named as 'Brad's Drink' from a soda fountain located at his pharmacy Bradham Drug Company in the city of New Bern situated at the confluence of Trent and Neuse rivers close to the sea beach of the south-east American state of North Carolina. Some 489 miles away from this place, 'Coca-Cola' had already taken birth seven years back in Atlanta (Georgia). Though both the drinks had contents of cola fruit, the two were different. While 'Pepsin enzyme' was used in Brad's Drink, 'Coca-Cola' had contents of 'coca leaves'. Coca leaves in Coca-Cola provided it a little bit of cocaine that triggered in the drinker a sense of energy boost associated with a feeling of exhilaration. On the other hand, pepsin enzyme in 'Brad's Drink' improved digestion as well as provided a sense of energy boost. There was a clear difference between the two drinks but by that time, Coca-Cola had established its identity in the market by promoting itself as the original/real beverage. That is why, when Bradham, in 1898, renamed his Brad's Drink to 'Pepsi-Cola' on the lines of Coca-Cola and started to promote the same also with the tagline 'The Original Food Drink', consumers had not taken it seriously. The majority of people considered Coca-Cola only as the original food drink and hence, they started treating 'Pepsi-Cola' as an imitation of Coca-Cola.

Not only that, until 1950, Pepsi-Cola had used 'price' only as the basis of its competition with Coca-Cola, as its managers considered that alone to be the best marketing strategy. This had badly damaged Pepsi-Cola's brand image and it got coined as 'kitchen cola', a cheap and the best alternative of the 'real cola'. However, starting from 1958, Pepsi focused on refining its brand image with its tagline 'Be Sociable, Have Pepsi', targeted at the younger generation. Again, starting 1961, Pepsi made attempts to make its brand image still more widespread with new ad slogan 'Now It Is Pepsi, For Those Who Think Young'. The two words 'Now' and 'Young' in the tagline had worked towards defining the features of Pepsi. The most interesting aspect of this tagline was that it had connected 'concept of youth' to the 'state of mind' instead of the 'real age'. This was also a correct brand strategy, as the brand Pepsi itself had already crossed the age of 60.

In fact, 1963 proved to be the real year to define the Pepsi brand when the company launched its 'Pepsi Generation' ad campaign. This campaign was also effective because the advertisements were based on mental attitude instead of price, quality, taste etc. of the product. However, it was the 'Pepsi Challenge' ad campaign of 1975 that had played the pivotal role in establishing the Pepsi brand. This campaign had not only challenged the customers by running a 'taste test' programme, but had also dared Coca-Cola openly to declare that Pepsi had a better taste. In the coming years, the 'Pepsi Challenge' campaign had created so much excitement and its communication had proved to be so effective that the same scared Coca-Cola and it had to modify its 'chemical formula' and launch 'New Coke' in the market. As Coca-Cola had always been a leading brand, its defensive strategy of being a 'follower' proved to be unsuccessful and 'New Coke' was badly beaten. As if Pepsi was just waiting for Coca-Cola to falter, it immediately launched its 'New Generation' ad campaign in an extremely aggressive manner. In this historical ad campaign, Pepsi had presented Michael Jackson when he was at the pinnacle of his popularity across the world.

Later, Pepsi had continued its campaign by securing appearance of other famous personalities. However, Pepsi's ad campaign in coordination with the 'Like a Prayer' album (1989) of Madonna had run into some controversies and it had to withdraw its campaign on account of boycott by its customers and criticism by the Vatican. However, the support from those personalities had overall helped Pepsi brand achieve huge success and it had established itself as the favourite brand of the youth in comparison to classic image of Coca-Cola. In recent years also, Pepsi has continued with its attempts to improve its brand image through innovative ad campaigns and it appears to be ready, with its differential identity, for every challenge from Coca-Cola.

Philip Morris/Marlboro: Marlboro is the world's largest selling cigarette brand. This is produced and distributed in the United States by Philip Morris USA (A company of Altria Group) and in other parts of the world by Philip Morris International (an independent company separate from Altria Group). At present, Marlboro is at the top position in the United States for the last 35 years, currently having 44% market share and its total sales being even more than combined sales of the rest of 10 American cigarette brands put together. 'Forbes' magazine had estimated its brand value as USD 21.90 billion with annual growth of 11% and had placed it at 26th position, one position up over previous year, among the 'World's Most Valuable Brands' of 2016. During that period, Marlboro had earned a revenue of USD 23.10 billion. As advertisements for tobacco products are largely banned across the world, Philip Morris had to spend USD 473 million only in 2015 to indirectly promote its 'Marlboro' brand.

Philip Morris, belonging to a German family living in England, had established his tobacco shop at Brand St. (road connecting Oxford St. in the north and Piccadilly in the south) in London in the year 1847. He had started producing cigarettes in his name in 1854; later in 1870, he had launched his cigarettes in the market with brand names 'Philip Morris Cambridge Blues' and 'Philip Morris Oxford Blues'. After his death in 1873, his widow Margaret Morris and nephew Leopold Morris carried on the trade and made the company public; the company was given the name 'Philip Morris & Company' in 1885. In 1894, the Morris family relinquished its control over the company and William Curtis Thomson and his family took over the same.

Again, in 1924, Philip Morris launched a new brand 'Marlboro', different from its own name; this was a high-quality brand targeted towards women. This name was picked up from the Great Marlborough St. (Soho, London) where the company had its factory earlier. Marlboro was promoted and marketed with the tagline 'Mild as May'. When scientists confirmed lung cancer to be a result of smoking during 1950s, Philip Morris had started to establish Marlboro as a cigarette for men. Till that time, filtered cigarettes were being marketed only for women, but now Marlboro was launched in the market with filter. In order to launch Marlboro in the market in its new form, the advertising agency in Chicago, Leo Burnett had launched a widespread ad campaign under which, captains of ships, weight-lifters, war journalists, construction workers etc. were presented as 'Marlboro Man' in a series of advertisements. The company management was initially hesitating to launch this campaign, but within a year of running this campaign, Marlboro brand hitherto having a market share of just 1%, jumped straight to the fourth position.

TV commercials were created in 1963 based on theme music of the film 'The Magnificent Seven',composed by American musician and music event organiser Almer Bernstein; however, after the ban was imposed on tobacco advertisements in 2006, the company started to promote 'Marlboro' brand by organising motor sports. If the sales of 'Marlboro' have gone up throughout the world despite limited advertisement options, it is only because of the legacy of the brand and exceptional quality of the product that attracts its fans.

Budweiser (Anheuser-Busch InBev Group): Budweiser, known as the 'King of Beers', is the largest selling (over 50%) pale lager brand of the United States. This is one of the 16 brands having sales of over USD 1 billion out of more than 200 alcohol brands produced and distributed by the world's largest alcohol-producing company (having over 25% share of the world market) Anheuser-Busch InBev (Leuven, Flemish Brabant, Belgium). This company was formed in 2007 through the amalgamation of three international alcohol-producing groups - Interbrew (Belgium), AmBev (Brazil) and Anheuser-Busch (USA). However, Anheuser-Busch (USA) had already introduced 'Budweiser' in American markets in 1876.

'Forbes' magazine had estimated the brand value of 'Budweiser' at USD 23.40 billion with an annual growth of 5%and had placed it at the 25th position among the 'World's Most Valuable Brands' of 2016. During the period, Budweiser had earned a revenue of USD 10.90 billion, but 'Forbes' has not provided any information on advertisement expenses incurred by the company.

Produced using barley and hops plants along with 30% rice, 'Budweiser' is a traditionally filtered beer that is served through fountain or offered in bottles or cans. Due to trademark controversies, this is sold in 80 countries of the world in different names. Though 'Budweiser' has been recording fall in its sales in the United States during the last few years, its total sales had gone up by 6.4% in 2014 on account of continuous growth in China, Russia and Brazil. The company pays a lot of attention to promotion of its brand, though no clear estimate is available on advertisement expenses for this specific brand.

Gillette (Proctor & Gamble/ P & G Group): Gillette is the leading brand in shaving and is world famous specifically for its safety razors. In January 2005, Proctor &Gamble (P&G) had acquired the Gillette Company established in 1901, along with its personal care products and various other brands through a share deal amounting to USD 57 billion. 'Forbes' magazine had estimated the brand value of Gillette at USD 20.20 billion with 1% annual decline and had placed the same down by 2 positions at 28th position among the 'World's Most Valuable Brands' of 2016. During that period, Gillette had earnedxc brand revenue of USD 7 billion, though for that, Proctor & Gamble (P&G) hadas\ to spend USD 8.30 billion, USD 1300 million more than the revenue, on advertisements for 'Gillette'. (Previous year also, to attain brand revenue of USD 7.90 billion for Gillette during 2014, P&G had to spend a total of USD 9.20 billion i.e. 1300 million extra.)

During the same period, P&G had spent a total of USD 8.30 billion on promotion and publicity of its baby care brand 'Pampers' and 'Pampers' was able to earn revenue (more compared to Gillette) of USD 10.40 billion. However, 'Forbes' magazine had estimated the value of 'Pampers' brand a USD 11.50 billion only (i.e. USD 8.70 billion less than that of Gillette) and placed the same at 50th position (22 places below Gillette) among the 'World's Most Valuable Brands' of 2016. However, the above figures present some interesting facts about Proctor & Gamble (P&G). P&G is the only company in the world that had spent USD 16.60 billion in a year to promote its two product brands.

In fact, it was during the summer of 1895 when the idea of developing a safety razor and a special kind of double-edged steel blade came up in the mind of the Boston (Massachusetts, USA) resident roving salesman King Camp Gillette, then working for Crown Cork & Seal Company, as he had got fed up with his straight razor. Camp Gillette had taken six years to perfect his ideal safety razor, as the machine tool makers that he had contacted had turned to be pessimistic and had termed his design to be impracticable. However, in 1901, Gillette finally teamed up with William Nickerson, an Massachusetts Institute of Technology (MIT)educated machine tools specialist, to turn his idea into a reality and founded 'The American Safety Razor Company'. In the beginning of 1903, it had started producing razors and blades, which were launched in the market in October through an advertisement published in 'Systems Magazine'. In the first year, a total of 51 razors and 168 blades were sold at the rates of USD 5 per razor and USD 1 per blade.

However, Camp Gillette was successful in getting patents registered in 1904 for his razor, blade and razor-blade set and sales had jumped to 90,884 razors and 1,23,648 blades during that year. Next year, the company had bought a six-storey building in south Boston area and had made payment of cash dividends to its investors for the first time in 1906. In the meantime, Gillette had started to expand his business in European countries by opening his first foreign sales centre in London in 1905. On the back of advertisements for his revolutionary razor and blade in various newspapers, Gillette was able to multiply his sales to such an extent that, by 1909, he had to install manufacturing plants in Paris (France), Montreal (Canada), Berlin (Germany) and Leicester (England) and expand his sales network. The American Army had placed an order for 3.50 million razors and 36 million blades during the First World War (1914 to 1918). Gillette had to engage 500 new employees to execute the order. In 1921, when the term of his patents had expired, Gillette had applied for a patent for an advanced version of the razor and had started selling the same at old prices.

Later, the Gillette Company had acquired other companies and expanded its presence in writing instruments (Paper Mate, Parker and Waterman brands), correction products (Liquid Paper brand), toothbrush and other oral hygiene products (Oral-B) and alkaline batteries (Duracell) also and had started selling its products in 200 countries after setting up 64 manufacturing facilities in 27 countries across the world. Thus, 60% of its sales were coming from outside the United States. However, only its razors and blades were the primary drivers of its business. In recent times, despite changes in customer behaviour with regard to shaving, Gillette has been successful in maintaining its business level on the strength of its innovative products and widespread promotion campaigns. As Gillette is now a part of P&G, clear figures relating to the business of this specific brand are not being made public.

Hershey Company: When there is a talk of chocolates, the first name that comes to mind of consumers is 'Hershey'. With a market share of 44.3%, the Hershey Company was the largest producer and seller of high-quality chocolates in the United States at the end of 2016, whereas its nearest competitor brand Marsh was lagging far behind with market share of just 29.3%. Of course, Marsh was at the top position in the American market of chocolate-free confectionery products with a market share of 18.2%, whereas Hershey was at the 2nd position with a market share of 13.5%. Hershey manages distribution and sale of its products with over 80 brand names in 70 countries. In the world market, Hershey is considered to be the 4th largest producer of chocolates after Mondelez (Cadbury), Marsh and Nestle. 'Forbes' magazine had estimated the brand value of Hershey at USD 6.7 billion with 7% annual growth and had placed the same at 99th position in the list of the 'World's Most Valuable Brands' of 2016. During that period, Hershey's revenue was USD 4.7 billion whereas the Hershey Company had spent USD 562 million on advertisements for its brands including 'Hershey'.

When Hershey's founder Milton Snavely Hershey dropped out of school at the age of 14, his mother had arranged for his apprenticeship with a local confectioner at Lancaster (Pennsylvania). During the next four years, Hershey learnt the art of making confectionery and started his first confectionery business in Philadelphia. Six years later, when his business had failed, Hershey apprenticed with a confectioner in Denver (now capital of Colorado state) and learnt to make caramel with fresh milk. After that, Hershey tried to establish his business in New York, but that attempt also failed. He then returned to Lancaster

(Pennsylvania) and founded Lancaster Caramel Company in 1886. The use of fresh milk in caramels proved to be successful. Hershey expanded his business quickly. Soon, 1400 employees started working for Lancaster Caramel Company and Hershey started exporting caramel to entire America as well as Europe.

In the meantime, an international exhibition, the World's Columbian Exposition was organised in Chicago in 1993. It was with this very exposition that the Chicago Parliament of Religions was convened where Swami Vivekananda had delivered his historic speech. Milton Snavely Hershey was so impressed after seeing German chocolate-making machines in the exhibition that he immediately bought two machines and sent them to Lancaster. Using some other equipment, Hershey started to create chocolate coating for his caramels. The ever growing demand for chocolates prompted Hershey to upgrade his entire production system to make the same capable of producing a unique concoction of milk chocolate. In 1894, when Hershey formally incorporated Lancaster Caramel Company, he also established Hershey Chocolate Company on 9 February 1994 as a subsidiary to the same.

During the next six years, Hershey found his milk chocolate business to be so promising that he sold his Lancaster Caramel Company in 1900 to American Caramel Company for USD 1 million (equivalent to approximately USD 287.88 million as on today). Hershey invested the entire amount in 'Hershey Chocolate Company' and started producing 'Hershey's Milk Chocolate Bar' brand. In 1903, Hershey started construction of a chocolate plant in his hometown Derry Church (Pennsylvania), which later came to be known as Hershey (Pennsylvania). This town was an inexpensive place for the workers and their families to live. The milk chocolate bars manufactured at this plant proved to be popular and the company grew rapidly.

Wrigley (Mars, Inc.): Whenever we talk of chewing gums, the first brand that comes to our mind is 'Wrigley'. William Wrigley Jr. had founded the 'Wm. Wrigley Jr. Company' on 1 April 1891 in the industrial city Chicago (Illinois) of the United

States of America. The American multinational confectionery group Mars Inc. had announced its acquisition on 28 April 2008 for USD 23 billion. It sells its products in more than 180 countries through its operational network in over 50 countries. It has 21 production facilities in 14 countries including the United States of America, Mexico, Spain, United Kingdom, France, Czech Republic, Poland, Russia, China, India, Japan, Kenya, Taiwan and Australia.

Wrigley's story is quite interesting. It was in 1891 when 29-year-old William Wrigley Jr. moved from Philadelphia to Chicago with just USD 32 with him and started a business to sell soaps. Wrigley started to offer his customers baking powder as free gift to improve sales of his soap. Wrigley was then aware that baking powder was more popular among people. He then started selling baking powder and to boost its sale, started offering chewing gum strips as free gifts. Very soon, Wrigley found out that the chewing gum was getting more popular. He thus concentrated on the manufacture of different kinds of chewing gums.

At that time, chewing gum was popular among women only. Soon, Wrigley offered two kinds of chewing gums in the brand names of 'Sweet Sixteen Orange' and 'Lotta Gum' targeted towards the youth market; this brought about a revolution in the entire chewing gum market. However, Wrigley tasted real success only when, during the economic slump in 1893, he brought out two other products with brand names 'Wrigley's Spearmint' and 'Juicy Fruit' that were going to become identities for the company. And when the economic downturn became still severe, William Wrigley Jr. took an unimaginable risky step. Wrigley pledged everything he owned and launched advertisement campaign on a large scale and very soon, Wrigley emerged as a national level company. Wrigley now understood the strategy of market expansion on the back of ad campaigns and he never had to look back after that.

Warren Buffett has always maintained that when an investor buys shares of stocks of these companies, he actually acquires ownership of a piece of the consumer's mind. The essence of Warren's observation is that when a company acquires ownership of the 'piece of consumers' minds', it never requires changing its products. In such a case, the company gets opportunities to realise better prices for its products as well as sell more products. Clearly, the company enjoys much better profit margin in that case and it achieves better inventory turnover; this is just like a big bottom line on income statement of the company. It is easy to identify such companies, as figures of their annual income are consistent and remain strong and debts are quite low or nil.

Warren asserts that these special kinds of companies providing durable competitive advantage present their managers the greatest opportunities for the best and the easiest growth in their professional lives. As such companies have fast cash flow, they are capable of making generous payments to their managers and employees towards their salary and various allowances as well as annual bonus. Not only that, these companies have plenty of funds to start new business and to acquire other companies to expand their business. Hence, young managers working for these companies also get great opportunities to excel in their professional lives.

Companies Selling Unique Services

Warren Buffett counts companies selling unique services also among the companies providing durable competitive advantage. Among such companies, he includes Moody's Corporation (business and financial services company), H & R Block (tax preparation company), American Express (financial services company), Service Master Global Holdings (residential and commercial services company) and Wells Fargo & Company (banking and financial services company).

Moody's Corporation: The name 'Moody' has been a synonym for securities for more than a century. This name has always been moulding itself to match the changing requirements of the American capital market Wall St. and financial markets across the world. Even this is interesting to note that while majority of the people in the world know about 'Moody's Investor Services' and its ratings and research reports, there are very few people who are aware of Moody's Corporation, a public company listed on the New York Stock Exchange. Yes, during 2016, Moody's Corporation was performing rating and analysis for 120 sovereign nations, around 11,000 corporations, 21,000 public financial services companies and 72,000 structured finance obligations through its offices and 11,700 employees in 36 countries. Moody's Corporation had reported revenue of USD 3.60 billion for the year 2016.

John Moody founded John Moody & Company in 1900 in New York, the financial capital of the United States, and published the first edition of 'Moody's Manual' that was full of statistics related to financial institutions, government establishments and companies listed on New York Stock Exchange. Within next few years, 'Moody's Manual' became a must-have for every investor and the company attained national reputation. John Moody then decided to publish books based on other financial matters through Moody Publishing Company. The first book 'The Truth About Trusts' was published in 1904; this contained details and analysis for public trusts in the United States. However, after the steep stock market crash of 1907, Moody and many of his loyal readers had to face suffering and he was compelled to sell his business along with his 'Moody's Manual'.

However, Moody returned with a new outlook within next two years. Moody's new approach was not just to provide information about companies to the investors worried about impending dangers but going a step further, to provide estimation of their assets and their performances also. Moody decided to address the fast-growing rail industries at that time and published a book titled 'Moody's Analysis of Railroad Investments' in 1909. In the book, Moody utilised the rating method followed by the then 'credit rating agencies', for in-depth analysis of rail industry. In 1912, Moody authored the book titled 'How to Analyse Railroad Reports' and in 1913, he widened his speciality beyond railroad industry to general financial ratings. Like his initial success,

Moody's professional expertise once again took him to a leading position in securities business. His ratings started getting popular among investors and in July 1914, he founded a new company named 'Moody's Investor Services'. During the next decade, Moody started to rates tocks as well as entire debt securities/ bond market. Moody authored many books for Yale University Press; two of those books published in 1919 - 'The Masters of Capital: A Chronicle of Wall Street' and 'Railroad Builders: A Chronicle of Welding of States' had been quite popular.

When in 1929, the share markets had crashed and the period of world recession had started, John Moody did not have to sell his business like before. Both he and his ever-growing 'rating services' survived. Despite collapse of many in the financial sector, Moody continued to write and publish his ratings and analysis results. He also wrote a memoir tilted 'The Long Road Home: An Autobiography' (McMillan, 1933), the next part of which was published with title 'Fast to The Road' (McMillan, 1942). John Moody breathed his last in February 1958 at the age of 89 years. Four years later, in 1962, Dun and Bradstreet, a major firm engaged in credit reporting and data collection, bought Moody's. During 1970s, Moody's started collecting fees from the companies getting rated. The time-taking in-depth research reports prepared by Moody's proved to be invaluable for both investors and the companies being analysed. Companies soon realised that getting a good rating from Moody's was just like having a good bank balance. Eventually, Dun and Bradstreet Corporation, having decided to take out Moody's services out of its private ownership spun off the same into a public traded company 'Moody's Corporation', listed on the New York Stock Exchange.

H&R Block: When an individual or a small businessman thinks of filing tax return, especially in the United States, the first name that flashes in his mind is that of H&R Block, the company providing specialised services in tax preparation; this company is however expanding its business to other countries of the world also. Yes, H&R Block also provides the same tax return filing services that your accredited chartered accountant does. However, it has been successful in developing this simple service as a specialised international brand and today, it is the largest tax services company in the world. In 2016, H&R Block was operating a total of 11,933 offices across the world; this included 10,223 offices (6,614 under company ownership and 3,599 as franchisees) in the United States, 1,282 in Canada, 438 in Australia and 5 in India. According to 'Forbes' magazine (May 2015), around 88,000 employees were working in these offices. During 2016, H&R Block had prepared a total of 2,31,68,000 tax returns (1,96,95,000 in the United States and 34,73,000 in other countries) and earned revenue of around USD 3 billion (with net profit of USD 374.20 million).

Henry Wollman Bloch, second son of a famous lawyer of Kansas City (the largest city of Missouri, a mid-west state of the United States), had joined Army Air Force services after completing his graduation from Michigan University; there, he was deputed to Harvard Business School for graduate training in statistical control. After returning from army services in 1946, Henry, along with his elder brother Leon, founded 'United Business Company' to offer tax return and book keeping services for common people and small professionals. However, as the business did not pick up in the first year, Leon left for seeking a law degree. Later, when the business picked up, Henry placed an advertisement to hire an employee. In response to the advertisement, his mother suggested him to hire his younger brother Richard who had just completed his graduation in economics from the Wharton School of Finance (Pennsylvania University). Both the brothers then started running the business; their business picked up slowly.

Henry and Richard placed an advertisement in local newspaper for their services and number of their clients started growing. When, in 1955, the Internal Revenue Service announced closure of their free service for tax return preparation, Henry placed an ad in a local newspaper and after that, there was sudden jump in the number of clients seeking tax preparation services. Finding the demand for their services growing, Henry Bloch renamed his company to 'H&R Block' that was easy to pronounce. The company business grew so rapidly that Henry went ahead to open seven offices in 1956; the company's revenue went up three times over previous year. In 1962, when the number of offices of the company had gone up to 206 and 'H&R Block' had become a national tax service brand, Henry made the company public and listed the same on the New York Stock Exchange.

American Express: American Express is known as an 'Integrity Brand'. 'Forbes' magazine had in May 2017 estimated the brand value of American Express at USD 24.50 billion with 1% growth and had placed the same at 23rd position in the list of the 'World's Most Valued Brands' of 2017. During that period, American Express had earned a revenue of USD 33.80 billion. However, the company had to also spend USD 3.7 billion on advertisements for brand promotion.

'American Express' has had a remarkable history. In 1850, it was founded as an express freight company and it earned its reputation and credibility by carrying out supplies to the eventual winners Union Army during the American Civil War (1861 to 1865). While continuing with its freight operations, American Express expanded its activities to financial service industry in 1980. Streams of European immigrants were at that time entering the United States and American Express offered them the service of making remittances to their home countries. In that course only, American Express in 1891 invented 'Travellers Cheque' that brought about revolution in travel as well as the finance industry.

However, another primary innovation emerged much later in 1958 in the form of 'American Express Card', a green coloured plastic charge card. Just like travellers' cheques, charge card also provided people an opportunity to get free from both eration of keeping cash in their pockets. As charge card could not be issued to all, very soon the 'American Express Card' became a status symbol among the American nobility. For the rest of the 20th century, American Express continued to run its ad campaign with tagline 'Membership Has Its Privileges' to promote this card. This tagline became quite famous and the elites across the world were clamouring for owning this card.

Though American Express has now grown to be a multinational company offering travel, financial and network services and promotes itself as a 'Financial Super Market', most of the people still consider it as a 'charge card' company only. As such, both 'American Express' brand and the card have changed their connotations during recent decades. This has continued to transform from an exclusive brand to an inclusive brand. In order to expand its customer base, the company started issuing 'credit card' also in addition to the charge card. Customers were buying this for practical convenience instead of as a status symbol. Though it was a very risky business strategy to transform from an 'Integrity Brand' to a 'Popular Brand', American Express has attained grand success in establishing itself as the 'World's Most Respected Service Brand' on the strength of its long experience and its unblemished and distinguished reputation for financial integrity and security. This is the reason that the company keeps on running widespread ad and mass-contact campaigns.

Service Master Global Holdings: Especially in the United States, 'Service Master' is regarded as the most popular brand for residential and commercial services. Service Master operates more than 7,000 company-owned and franchisee branches around the world. It has 13,000 corporate employees whereas the franchisee network independently employs around 33,000 additional people. The core services of the company include termite and pest control, home warranty, disaster response and restoration, janitorial service, home cleaning, furniture repair and home inspection. During 2016, Service Master Global Holdings earned a net profit of USD 155 million on total revenue of USD 2.746 billion.

The founder of Service Master, Marion E. Wade had to drop out of his 8th standard and take up the job of a peon to help his family. Along with that, he continued to play baseball and even joined the semi-professional team of 'Chicago Braves' in 1915. After the death of his brother during the First World War, Wade joined the US Navy in 1918 and even underwent combat training. However, the War was soon over. A few days after returning from the services, Wade married in 1920 and leaving baseball, he started his professional life as a sales person. Nine years later, when the period of great recession had begun in 1929, Wade started providing moth proofing services for residences and offices. Some 18 years later, in 1947, Wade incorporated 'Wade, Wagner & Associates' and started offering carpet-cleaning services also in addition to moth proofing. The business picked up rapidly and in 1954, Wade renamed his company to 'Service Master'.

After the death of Wade in 1973, his successors took the business forward. In July 2007, a group of private equity investment firms led by Clayton, Dubilier and Rice (CD&R) acquired Service Master. In June 2014, the company with name 'Service Master Global Holdings' was incorporated as a publicly traded company and listed on the New York Stock Exchange.

Wells Fargo & Company: 'Wells Fargo' is a major financial services brand of the world. In May 2017, 'Forbes' magazine had estimated its brand value at USD 13.2 billion with 4% growth and had placed the same at 43rd position in the list of the 'World's Most Valuable Brands' of 2017. During that period, Wells Fargo had earned a revenue of USD 94.2 billion and the company had spent USD 595 million on brand promotion.

In the list of the 'World's 2000 Largest Public Companies' of 2017, 'Forbes' magazine had placed Wells Fargo at fifth position after Industrial and Commercial Bank of China (ICBC), China Construction bank, Berkshire Hathaway and JP Morgan Chase; at that time, its total sales amounted to USD 97.60 billion, profit USD 21.90 billion, assets USD 1,943.40 billion and market capitalisation USD 274.40 billion. It may be noted that on 22 July 2015, Wells Fargo & Company attained the status of the world's largest financial institution by surpassing Industrial and Commercial Bank of China (ICBC) with a market capitalisation of USD 301.60 billion, and then, its market price was USD 40 billion above that of JP Morgan and USD 120 billion above that of Citi Group. Not only that, Wells Fargo had beaten ICBC even in 2013.

In the beginning of 1848, when gold was found at Sutter's Mill near Coloma (California), entrepreneurs and financiers from all over North America and the world had flocked to California, drawn by the promise of huge profits. Vermont native Henry Wells and New Yorker William G. Fargo had also then watched the California economy boom with keen interest; but, as they were so busy with their profitable businesses at that time,they did not show any hurry to rush there. However, they founded Wells Fargo & Company on 18 March 1852 with an initial capital of USD 0.30 million, to provide banking services in California. After going through all the ups and downs, the present Wells Fargo & Company took birth in 1998 by merger with Norwest Corporation. As Wells Fargo enjoyed a historical brand image, that very name was carried forward.

For the above companies, the economics of selling unique services may be extraordinary. Such companies have to neither modify or replace the design of their products nor spend money on installation of production units. They have to spend a major part of their fortune on constant upgradation of plant and machinery and on godowns to store their products. Not only that, these companies that provide unique services and possess ownership of a part of the mind of the consumers, are able to generate better profit margin as compared to the companies selling products. Obviously, the managers who work for these companies enjoy much higher remunerations. Their professional lives are more productive and stable, as such companies do not have to face the financial ups and downs that impact other businesses badly.

Now, if we examine the operating histories of companies like H&R Block and General Motors, we may notice that, irrespective of severity of economic slump, the business of tax return preparation never faces any slowdown, as people, in any case, are required to file their tax returns. On the contrary, even an economic slump for a short period may damage the financial condition of companies like General Motors, as people stop buying motor vehicles. Not only that, the managers and directors of companies like H&R Block do not have to burn midnight oil as those in companies like General Motors do, worrying either for the demands of the workers unions or increasing debts or sudden changes in consumers' behaviour.

Companies Trading At Low Costs

According to Warren Buffett, the third kind of companies that provide durable competitive advantage are those who buy things at very low costs and sell them to consumers at the lowest prices. Among Warren's such favourite companies are Walmart, Costco, Nebraska Furniture Mart, Borsheims Fine Jewelry and Burlington Northern Santa Fe. These companies are successful in keeping their profit margins high due to high volumes of sales. As these companies make purchases at large scale, their costs are low and hence, they are able to achieve high sale volumes and good profit margins at the lowest prices as compared to their competitors. The lowest prices become goodwill for these companies and keep attracting consumers to their stores.

Walmart Stores: Walmart is a 'scale business' brand. During the period between 1980s and 90s, Walmart, besides expanding in regional markets of the United States, had established its dominance on national level also. By 1988, Walmart had become the highest profit earning and by October 1989, the highest revenue earning retail stores chain of the United States. In 2002, Walmart had become the largest company of the United States by earning a net profit of USD 6.70 billion on total revenue amounting to USD 219.80 billion. By earning a net profit of USD 15.40 billion on total revenue of USD 422 billion (that included contribution of 109.20 billion from international operations) for the year ending 31 January 2011, Walmart had secured the position of the world's largest company (in terms of revenue).

In May 2017, 'Forbes' magazine estimated Walmart's brand value at USD 24.10 billion and placed the same at 24th position in the list of the 'World's Most Valuable Brands' of 2017. During that period, Walmart had earned a revenue of USD 326.30 billion, the highest among all in the list, and had spent USD 2.90 billion on its advertisements. For the year ending 31 January 2017, Walmart Stores had earned net profit of USD 14.293 billion on total revenue of USD 485.873 derived through a huge network of 11,500 stores operating under 65 trade names in 28 countries of the world. In the list of the 'World's Largest Public Companies' of 2017, 'Forbes' magazine placed Walmart Stores at the 9th position in the overall category, first position in sales revenue, 11th position in net profit, 35th position in assets and 15th position in market capitalisation category.

The interesting fact is that it was in 1945 when 27 years old Sam Walton started Walmart as a simple retail business. Then, how did this grow into the world's largest retail brand and the world's largest revenue earning company? Sam Walton has mentioned in his biography 'Made in America - My Story' that his strong resolve to connect with the customers was at the core of his business philosophy. In his list of 'Business Building Rules', Walton has written in his 8th rule –'Let them (your customers) know you appreciate them.' Yes, Walmart implements this in its business in many ways. Despite being huge in size, Walmart has always tried to provide its customers a homely atmosphere, treat them as neigh bours and develop personal rapport with them. For measuring customers' spending pattern, Walmart has been utilising specialised high-grade software right from its initial phase, and on the basis of the information coming out of the same, the suppliers of Walmart were able to find out the items, their quantities and the stores where the same were required to be supplied.

However, the key to Walmart's success is the scale of its business. Walmart, on account of huge size of its stores, makes all possible efforts through its 'store receptionists' to turn the buying experience of every customer personal. It is because of its size only that Walmart is able to buy any product in large quantity at minimum cost and sell the same at minimum price.

It is Walmart's size only that enables it to offer its customers 'Every Day Low Prices' i.e., items offered at the minimum sale price in comparison to any other store. Walmart has always kept on growing in size and moving ahead. This is the reason that Walmart has not been able to get permission for direct retail business in many countries, including India. The Government of India is concerned that Walmart's entry into retail business might sound the death knell for small and medium retailers. However, Walmart cannot abandon its customer-centric business philosophy just for that.

Nebraska Furniture Mart: Nebraska Furniture Mart (NFM) is the largest home furnishing store of North America. Located at South 72nd St. in Warren Buffett's hometown Omaha (Nebraska), its main store has retail space extending to 4,20,000 square feet (39,000 sq. m) within a 77-acre (3,10,000 sq. m) single collective campus. Nebraska Furniture Mart was founded by Rose Blumkin, popularly known as Mrs. B., in 1937. Though, at the age of 89 years, Mrs. B. sold 80% stake in Nebraska Furniture Mart, amounting to USD 60 million, to Warren Buffett in 1983, she continued, at Buffett's request, to manage the store almost for her entire life.

Rose Blumkin was born on 3 December 1893 in Schedrin, a village near Minsk (capital of Belarus). She was one among eight children of Solomon and Chasya Gorelick. His father was religious teacher in Judaism (rabbi) and her mother ran a grocery store to support her struggling family. All the siblings had to sleep on straw in a single room. Rose used to feel pity for his father's prayers who was not capable of even providing a mattress to his family. When her mother had to bake breads in oven in the night like slaves, she used to get awake at midnight. She would feel quite distressed to see her mother toiling and hence, right from the age of 6, she had started assisting her mother in running her retail store. The Gorelick couple did not have enough money to send their children for school education. In the circumstances, Rose did not get a chance to attend any class in a school, but she learnt reading, writing and counting in an affluent family. The greatest lesson she learnt from her mother was that begging was the most despicable job. This was the reason that, right at the age of 13 years, Rose took up a job at a dry goods store in Minsk. Three years later, when she was 16 years old, Rose became manager of the store with six male employees reporting to her.

When Rose was twenty, she married shoe salesman Isador Blumkin, who soon thereafter immigrated to the United States in order to avoid conscription in Russian Army. Rose also had then thought that she would soon join her husband in the United States. But, the War started before she could leave. Later, during the unbearable cold of 1917, when Europe was burning and Russia was trembling, Rose boarded the Trans-Siberian Railway (the world's largest railway network from Moscow to Vladivostok - connecting Lake Baikal and the far-east region of Russia in East Siberia and touching the borders of Mongolia, China and North Korea). The Russian security forces detained Rose at the border region of China, as she did not possess a passport. Rose told the Russian security forces that she was going to buy leather for army and she would bring bottles of vodka for them while returning. Thus, she reached Japan after crossing Manchuria in northeast China; there, she secured a place on a ship and some six weeks later, she somehow managed to get down at Seattle port (United States). Though Rose could not speak English, she was successful in locating her husband Isador Blumkin in Fort Dodge, Iowa.

Later, the Blumkin couple relocated to Omaha (Nebraska) in 1919. Isador opened a used clothing store and Rose started selling furniture from its basement. Though they themselves were quite poor, Rose asked her parents and siblings to join them and they all were living together under the same roof. As Rose could not speak English, her children taught her English after they started going to school. In 1937, when she was 44, Rose managed to save USD 500 and she took a store on rent on Furnam St. Rose had big dreams and hence, she named her store as 'Nebraska Furniture Mart'. Her way of selling and her motto - both were the same - 'Sell cheap and tell the truth'. Branded furniture houses found Rose Blumkin's way of selling detrimental to their businesses and hence, they stopped supplies to her; however, Rose was expert in selling illegitimate goods. She would go to Chicago or Kansas where retailers like Marshal Field would sell their extra items at prices just a little over their cost. This way, Rose Blumkin continued to sell furniture at the lowest prices.

Rose had applied for a loan for expansion of her business, but bank officials ridiculed her and rejected her request. This experience developed an everlasting sense of hatred in her mind towards so-called 'big people'; however, she, on the strength of her unwavering resolve, carried forward her business ideal. She continued working for 7-days a week, 52-weeks a year without taking leave even for a day. Yes, Rose Blumkin had affection with her work and her middle-class consumers. These loyal customers would come to this very store for their entire home furnishing needs and gradually, Rose Blumkin became popular among them as 'Mrs. B'.

In 1949, Mohawk Carpet Mills dragged her to court alleging violation of 'fair trade law' by her. As a manufacturer, Mohawk had fixed the minimum retail price for its carpet at USD 7.25 per yard, but 'Mrs. B' was selling the same at the rate of USD 4.95. The judge in fact asked the lawyer of Mohawk, "Then, what's wrong in that?" and rejected their charge. Not only that, that judge himself visited Nebraska Furniture Mart next day and bought carpets for USD 1,400.

Next year, when 'Mrs. B' was unable to make payments to her suppliers, one of her friends, a bank officer, extended a loan of USD 50,000 for 90 days. Mrs. B had then taken a big risk to keep her business afloat on any condition. She rented a big conference hall and sold furniture amounting to USD 2.50 in the next three days and took a pledge never to borrow again. Thus, at the age of 57, 'Mrs. B' had started running her business entirely in her own way.

'Mrs. B' also used to treat her workers and her family members quite mercilessly. However, Mrs. B's eldest son, Louis also was a hardworking businessman like his mother. Contrary to his mother, he was a very gentle and soft-natured person. Thus, whenever Mrs. B fired a worker, he would employ him again. This way, Louis used to save his mother from her mistakes. But, Mrs. B's business principle was so attractive and tempting that customers were not able to stop themselves from coming to Nebraska Furniture Mart. She would make purchases in large quantities, keep her costs to the minimum and try to pass on all her saving to the customers. Normally, she used to sell her items at prices just 10% more than her costs; however, she was famous for creating exceptions. She would instantly reduce prices depending on customers' needs and their pockets and sell items at just their wholesale prices.

As such, Warren Buffett was desirous of acquiring Nebraska Furniture Mart for a long time; but it was a privately owned company. However, when Buffett put forward his proposal for acquisition in 1983, Louis and his three sons were managing the store and 'Mrs. B' was the chairperson of the company and fulltime administrator of its carpet section. When Buffett learnt that she was willing to sell the store, he went through the tax return of the store. The store's pre-tax income at that time was USD 15 million. Warren did not make any enquiry about the assets of the store and offered Mrs. B the proposal for 80% ownership for a value of USD 60 million, that was five times its income, and Mrs. B immediately accepted the same. It may be noted that Nebraska Furniture Mart was having annual sales of USD 100 million at that time and it had two-thirds share in total furniture sales in Omaha. Even the furniture store chain like D Lords that was grossing annual sales of USD 4 billion had not opened its store in Omaha only for the reason that it was not in a position to compete with the prices offered by 'Mrs. B'. This was the reason that, even after acquisition, Warren Buffett left the management of the store with Mrs. B and her family only. However, in 1989, when her family members forced 'Mrs.

B' into retirement at the age of 95, she was quite upset with their decision and just after three months, she opened "Mrs. B's Clearance & Factory Outlet" just in front of the store. Mrs. B's new store came into profit within next two years and it grew to be the third largest furniture store of Omaha. The following year, Warren Buffett bought this store also and got it merged with the old store.

In 1994, Nebraska Furniture Mart added an electronic and home appliance store also. In 1998, when 'Mrs. B' died at the age of 104, she had left behind the largest furniture store of the United States. In 2001, the Mart acquired 'Homemakers Furniture' and opened its second store in Iowa; in 2003, the Mart opened its third store in Kansas. By 2011, the business attitude had changed and in 2013, Nebraska Furniture Mart opened its fourth and the largest store in The Colony (Texas).

Borsheims Jewelry Company: Warren Buffett was so impressed by the business style of Mrs. B that just six years after acquisition of Nebraska Furniture Mart, he had acquired Borsheims Jewelry located in Omaha . Louis Borsheims had founded this jewellery store in 1870; but, when Mrs. B's sister Rebecca and brother-in-law Louis Friedman purchased that small jewellery store in 1948, they also adopted her motto 'Sell cheap and tell the truth' and the store started gaining popularity rapidly.

In 1986, when they found the 116-years old 8000 sq. ft. Borsheims store, located in Omaha city centre, to be too small, it was relocated to a 23,000 sq. ft. facility at Regency Court, the most expensive shopping centre in Omaha. Very soon, Borsheims had grown to be the largest selling jewellery store, after Tiffany & Company, of the United States. Later, Borsheims further expanded its retail space to 62,500 sq. ft., adding large watch section, gift gallery and jewellery repairs and design facility to the same. More than 100,000 jewellery items, watches and gifts were displayed in the store. Borsheims Jewelry Company meets demands of its international customers spread across 50 countries through this sole facility.

Burlington Northern Santa Fe Corporation: This is the parent company of the BNSF Railway (formerly the Burlington Northern Santa Fe Railway). This corporation was incorporated in 1993 to facilitate the merger of Burlington Northern and Santa Fe Pacific Corporation. The BNSF Railway is one of the largest freight railroad networks in North America. It has 44,000 employees, 32,500 miles (52,300 km) of track in 28 states and more than 8000 locomotives. It has three transcontinental routes that provide rail connections between the western and the eastern Unites States.

On 3 November 2009, Berkshire Hathaway had offered its proposal to buy the remaining 77.4% share in Burlington Northern Santa Fe Corporation for a value of USD 26 billion. Considering the earlier investment of Berkshire and USD 10 billion of loans and other liabilities of Burlington Northern, this deal was finalised for USD 44 billion. Concluded on 12 February 2010, this was the largest acquisition in the history of Berkshire Hathaway.

In this chapter, we have till now discussed three kinds of business models that provide durable business advantage. Out of them, the low-cost trading companies provide minimum opportunities for career advancement. As the managements of these companies are always under pressure to keep the costs to the minimum, they try to maintain their employees' emoluments also at a low level. Still, compared to other average grade businesses, these companies offer better opportunities for jobs and management. Warren Buffett considers the companies working in all these three business models to be 'right businesses'. However, he also performs economic tests of the concerned companies to pick the best out of them.

❑

2

Economic Test of a Business

As we have read in the previous chapter, in Warren Buffett's point of view, only those companies can be the best for ownership, investment and working that are capable of providing the greatest opportunities for career advancement, job security and long-term earnings. Warren considers such a company only the 'right business' able to provide 'durable competitive advantage', as the inherent business economics of the company works in its favour. In the previous chapter, we have learnt about three business models of the companies providing 'durable competitive advantage' and we will now discuss the methods that Warren Buffett uses to perform the economic test for those companies.

It may be noted that Warren Buffett had always considered investing as a pure business. This concept or philosophy of investing is called 'business perspective investing' in professional language. In Buffett's view, the real investment is the one that follows the fundamental principles of business and there is no place for conjecture or speculation in the same. The primary aim of a business is to earn profit that operates on the basic formula of economics of demand and supply. The mystery of the historical investment Buffet's success is implied in this very 'business perspective investing'. This phrase may appear to be simple but it is a very challenging concept. It is not because investing with business approach requires superlative financial and accounting knowledge, but because this is entirely different from the prevalent wisdom of the capital market.

Warren Buffett's concept of 'business perspective investing' is a special kind of professional skill that is based more on business discipline that on 'business philosophy' and once you are able to understand this concept, you would know that this skill also demands absolute devotion. This absolute devotion helps you to maintain your existence in financial landscape. Even a minor deviation would force you to dance to the tune of senseless concepts of 'fear' and 'greed' and, you would never be a prudent investor and would turn into an imprudent speculator forever.

Please keep in mind that all the capital markets in the world have large numbers of imprudent speculators who help create atmosphere of fear and greed by fanning silly business behaviour based on conjecture. People having dreams of getting rich quick get caught in their net, as they find this route of speculation easy. Such people are never able to enjoy the strenuous practice of prudent investors and become a part of the large team of speculators or withdraw from the market itself after losing everything. On the contrary, if you invest with the perspective of business, others' stupidity becomes a fertile land for you to harvest the crop of profit; that means imprudent speculators in capital markets indulge in silly business behaviour because of the widely popular mentality of fear and greed whereas prudent investors, who only make disciplined and prudent investments with business perspective, get opportunities to make profits out of their mistakes. Hold on! Prudent investors making investments with business perspective do not get profit-making opportunities only from others' silliness. In fact, they are able to enjoy these profit-making opportunities created by others' mistakes just because of their disciplined business behaviour.

In order to adopt Warren Buffett's fundamental investment philosophy based on business perspective, we will have to definitely learn the art of evaluating a business or else, our investment decisions would not be prudent and we also would join the team of the gamblers of the capital markets and get entangled in speculations. And, in order to determine the condition of any business entity, its business balance sheet will have to be analysed and the meaning behind its figures will have to be understood thoroughly.

Warren Buffett's 'Pinball' Business

Keep in mind that,before starting his business, young Warren Buffett had never thought that he would grow to be the richest person of the United States or the world. He did not have any such dreams also. Yes, he was definitely eager right from his childhood to earn a lot of money and for that, he had decided to start a business. As he wanted to reap the amazing benefits of compound interest fully, he was also fully aware that the sooner he started his business the better would be its results. He was also aware that it would not be possible to earn compound interest after death; instead, the tax department would be at the door for recoveries.

In fact, Warren had started displaying his inborn interest in business and investing at a young age. In his childhood itself, he had started making money by selling chewing gums and Coca-Cola bottles and delivering weekly magazines door-to-door. He had also worked in his grandfather's grocery store. While still in high school, he had already made good money by selling golf balls and stamps, cleaning cars and delivering newspapers. In 1944, when he filed his first income tax return, he had reported his income after claiming deduction for use of his bicycle and watch for newspaper delivery.

In 1945, as a high school sophomore, he had made a lot of research on high-income businesses. And finally, he bought a used pinball machine (special kind of coin-operated amusing game machine) in good working condition for US$ 35. Thus, he had created the first asset for his business and now, to install the machine, he was looking for a site where maximum people could use the same. He first of all contacted the local billiard hall operator who told him that he already had four pinball machines. In fact, he did not want Warren also to install his machine there and break his customers. Hence, he turned Warren away. Warren was then able to figure out that the billiard hall operator had created his monopoly over indoor games in the local market and he did not want anybody else to enter that field.

Naturally, for Warren Buffett who was already impatient to start his business, this was his first encounter with the market reality. And, he did get highly frustrated with this shock depriving him the opportunity to make money. But he was not ready to accept defeat. As he had already made a complete analysis of the profitability of the business even before buying the pinball machine, there was no question of going back. He was determined to use this business to make money. He had also understood well that the most important factor affecting the success of a retail business was - its location. Access to the location that had the maximum movement of customers was in any case denied to Warren. Hence, Warren started looking for other options. Very soon, a great idea clicked in his mind. He observed that most of the youth playing pinball sported 'crew cut' hair. He then found out that alocal barber named 'Searge' was offering that style of haircut.

When Warren inspected Searge's barber shop, he found out two things - firstly, there was no pinball machine there and secondly, the shop had a large space where the youth willing to play pinball could wait for their turn. Then itself, the idea of the first joint venture of his life clicked in Warren's mind and he offered Searge the proposal to share 20% of total revenue if he permitted him to set up his pinball machine in the shop. As if Searge was waiting for such an offer, he immediately said 'yes' to Warren. Very next day, Warren installed the pinball machine there. Next day, when Warren went to the shop, he found US$

10 in the machine. He gave 20% share (USD 2) to Searge and pocketed 80% of revenue (USD 8). While coming out of the shop, Warren realised that this business was going to be quite lucrative.

But it is complicated to answer what would be the valuation of Buffett's pinball business. We will have to study the economics of the business.

Study of Balance Sheet: To study the economics of a business, we need to first of all look at its balance sheet i.e., its financial condition. (See table)

One-day Balance Sheet of Pinball Business

Assets	
Cash (from a day's operation)	$ 8.00
Property	$ 35.00
Total Assets	$ 43.00
Liabilities	
Debts	$ 0.00
Paid-up Capital (Money used to start business)	$ 35.00
Retained Income (Money retained out of business operations)	$ 8.00
Shareholders Equity / Book Value	
Paid-up Capital + Retained Income	$ 43.00
Total Shareholders Equity & Liabilities	
	$ 43.00

In fact, a balance sheet is the report of financial position of a company. The one-day balance sheet of Warren Buffett's pinball business reveals that his total assets amount to USD 43 and he does not have any liabilities. We can see under assets category a figure of USD 8 that represents amount collected from a day's operation and property of USD 35 that represents the value of the pinball machine. As Warren has not taken any loan for his business, he does not even have any liabilities. Paid-up capital is the amount that was used to start the business, and here, that amount is USD 35. Retained income is the amount kept out of income from business operations and in this case, USD 8 is the amount generated after a day's operation. The total of paid-up capital and retained income is shareholders equity that is also called book value or net worth and here, that amount is USD 43 (35 + 8).

It may be noted that we may create balance sheet for our business as on any date, but incorporated units/companies prepare the same at the end of fiscal/financial quarters and financial year.

Study of 'Income Statement: Another important document for evaluation of any business is – the income statement. Income statement for one-day operation of Warren's pinball business would be prepared as below.

One-day Income Statement for Pinball Business

Revenue	$ 10.00
Expenses	$ 2.00
Income	$ 8.00

Revenue is the amount generated by business operations or other sources. Here, one day's operation has generated USD 10.00 that represents its one-day revenue. As there is no income from any other sources, hence the same is not reflected above. 'Expenses' represents the amount that is spent to operate the business and in the above case, Warren made a payment of USD 2 to Searge and the same is categorised under expenses. Thus, business income amounts to USD 8 that Warren could pocket.

Evaluation of Pinball Business: Till now, we have studied his one-day balance sheet and income statement to evaluate Warren Buffett's pinball business. Then, what would be the value of this business? The balance sheet shows the book value or networth as USD 43. Does this mean the value of the company is just USD 43? Or, is it possible that Warren Buffett would have sold his business at this price? Clearly, Warren would have never done this and if the business belonged to you, you also would not have done this, as it had the potential to make an average net income or profit of USD 8.

As Searge's barber shop remained open on all seven days of the week, even on holidays, the business was to run on all 365 days of a year. Also, as Searge's customers were not going to go anywhere else for haircut and they would have waited for their turn in that hall where Warren had installed the pinball machine, at least that many people would have definitely used the machine to result in average daily revenue of USD 10. Further, as Searge was also receiving his 20% share in income, he was going to take proper care of the machine and also encourage his customers to use the same. Hence, the possibility of profit was definite. Thus, at the rate of USD 8 per day, this business was going to earn profit of USD 2,920 per year ($8 x 365 days). Had somebody bought the business at USD 43 of shareholders equity or book value or net worth, he would have made a profit of USD 2,920 before corporate income tax, at the end of first year. This way, the investors would have got an opportunity to achieve a great return on investment.

Was Warren a fool then that he would have sold his business with such a potential to an investor for just USD 43 of shareholders equity or book value or net worth? Definitely not! Warren would have affirmed that his pinball business was going to make annual profit of USD 2,920; he expected the business to run at the same level for next ten years and hence, the buyer would have got an opportunity to make a total profit of USD 29,200 in next ten years. Does this mean Warren would have indicated the present value of his business to that buyer as USD 29,200? Absolutely not! Because, the buyer of the business could have enjoyed opportunities to make USD 44,516 out of the profits from this business. But how? This was possible if the business profits were invested regularly in a bank's recurring deposit or money market fund earning average 8% interest.

Then, how would have the buyer evaluated Warren's business? It is clear that Warren had estimated the future value of his business as USD 44,516, assuming the buyer regularly invested daily income of USD 2,920 ina deposit account or any other financial product earning 8% interest. Thus, had the buyer decided to buy Warren's business assuming 8% annual return on his investment, he would have estimated its present value as USD 20,619.52 approximately.

It would be better if you use a financial calculator for this computation, as manual computation of compound interest may take a lot of time. You may even use financial calculator for this, but it is costly. Hence, you better use financial calculators available on the Internet. There are separate calculators for future value and present value. For now, in the present value calculator, write $ 44,516 in the space for FV (future value), 10 in the space for N (number of years) and 8% in the space for I/Y (interest per year) and click on 'Calculate' button. The result you get would be - 20,619.52.

Had the buyer paid the present value USD 20,619.52 for Warren's pinball business, it would have meant that he expected a return of 8% compound interest on his investment and he found it appropriate to receive a future value of USD 44,516 at the end of 10th year. This would have also meant that the buyer did not have any other investment option that could have generated a better return. Would he have accepted Warren's sale offer if he had another investment option giving 10% compound interest? Definitely not! Then, what would have he estimated as the present value of Warren's pinball business? In the present value calculator, leave all the values as entered earlier and change the value for I/Y (Interest per year) from 8% to 10% and click 'Calculate' button. You will get the answer as - $17,165.85. This means that the buyer would have got an opportunity to earn a total interest amount of USD 27,353.15 on his purchase price of USD 17,162.85 at @10% pa.

Then, what should be the real value of Warren's pinball business? According to Warren, at least USD 20,619.52.

However, the final value depends on the fact whether the buyer is ready to buy at that price. If the buyer has a risk-free option to earn better return on his investment, he would not buy the same at that price. He would try to look for another option at USD 17,162.85 to earn compound interest @10% pa. Clearly, if you evaluate any investment proposal this way, you can find out its appropriate present value. And, from the point of view of Warren, remember the first lesson of investment - the price one pays eventually determines the return of investment. The lower the purchase price, the higher will be the profit. Only the investors who take their investment decision this way are considered to be 'prudent investors' by Warren Buffett; those indulging in guesswork are called speculators.

Earn Compound Interest, Get Rich

Since, Warren Buffett was very, amazed by compound interest, he would always explain its amazing beneficial results to his initial partners. The history of the phenomenal success of the Berkley Hathaway, company that manages Warren Buffett's investment empire, presents an exceptional example of the 'miracle of compound interest'.

Berkley Hathaway was established in 1839 as the Valley Falls Company in Cumberland (Rhode Island, the United States of America). In 1962, Warren had started buying shares of Berkley Hathaway through his partnership investment company. During the initial months of 1965, he had amassed 49% shares and on 10 May 1965, he had even acquired the company. Though Warren had started buying the shares @ USD 7.60 per share, the average buying cost for all the shares ultimately came out to be USD 14.86 per share. At that time, the value of each share on the basis of book value of Berkley Hathaway was estimated to be around USD 19.

As Warren, from the start itself, wanted to earn compound interest, he had persuaded all his partners for a long-term investment. That was the reason that he neither allowed his original shares (Class-A) to get split nor issued any dividends.

Thus, in the initial 25 years, Berkley Hathaway, listed on New York Stock Exchange, saw its share price jump more than 373 times to a level of USD 7,100 (1 June 1990). Five years later, in 1995, the average market price of Berkley Hathaway's share had gone over USD 22,000, much beyond the reach of most of the investors. Considering market demand for higher accessibility and liquidity, Berkshire Hathaway issued shares under class-B category on 9 May 1996; average investors then got the privilege to include this reputed company in their portfolios. However, the stock right of a class-B share was just 1/1,500 and voting right 1/10,000 as compared to a class-A share.

It may be kept in mind that the company never issued dividends except in 1967, as Warren Buffett had invested shareholders' money in more profitable enterprises. This resulted in steady increase in the price of Berkshire Hathaway's share, rising to USD 2,66,013 as on 1 March 2017. Thus, during 52 years from 1965 to 2017, Berkley Hathaway's share price has gone up 14,000 times.

Warren Buffett had been always telling his partners that the perfect way to get rich in real sense was to earn maximum compound interest on their investments. Warren's investment strategy based on compound return can be understood easily with the help of the following table.

Compound Return on Investment of USD 1,00,000

Period/ Interest Rate	5%	10%	15%	20%
10 years	$ 1,62,889	$ 2,59,374	$ 4,04,555	$6,19,173
20 years	$ 2,65,329	$ 6,72,749	$ 16,36,653	$ 38,33,759
30 years	$ 4,32,194	$ 17,44,940	$ 66,21,177	$ 2,37,37,631

Thus, if USD 1,00,000 is invested for 10 years with compound interest rate of 5% pa, we can get a return of USD 162,889. If the rate of compound interest is increased by 5% (i.e. 10%), the return goes up to USD 2,59,374. And if the rate of compound interest is 20%, we may get an opportunity to receive a return of USD 6,19,173 on investment of USD 1,00,000. And, if we continue our investment at compound interest rate of 20% for 30 years, it is possible to even get the maximum return of USD 2,37,37,631. Yes, it was because of this very strategy of Warren Buffett that it was possible for Berkshire Hathaway's per share book value or net worth to grow at an average rate of 20.3% during the period of 45 years from 1965 to 2009.

However, another aspect of Warren Buffett's mystery of the magic of compound interest is that, by not issuing dividends, he saved a lot of personal taxes for the investors. To understand this, let's have a look at the table below showing 'Compound Return on Earned & Retained Profits (8%)'.

Compound Return on Earned & Retained Profits (8%)

Year	Invested Amount	Earned & Retained Interest
1	$ 1,000.00	$ 80.00
2	$ 1,080.00	$ 80.40
3	$ 1,166.40	$ 93.31
4	$ 1,259.71	$ 100.77
5	$ 1,360.48	$ 100.83
Total		**$ 469.31**

Assuming that a person puts USD 1,000 intoan investment offer of a company providing 8% annual return, he may get an opportunity to earn a compound return of USD 469.31 at the end of the 5th year if the company, instead of paying dividend at the end of each year, keeps retaining the earned interest and reinvesting the same. After paying a minimum 33% (2017) i.e., USD 154.87 towards personal income tax on this dividend income of USD 469.31, the investor will be left with the real return of USD 314.43 (469.31 - 154.87) on his investment of USD 1,000.

However, an investor can achieve the same only if he invests in shares of a company that, instead of paying him annual dividend, retains the same and invests it in investment options providing better returns. Warren had done the same. He had retained annual dividends of Berkshire Hathaway's investors and invested the same in more profitable options. As Warren did not make dividend payments to his investors, they did not have to pay income tax on the same every year. Berkshire Hathaway had reinvested those dividend amounts in more profitable options; the price of the company's share was hence constantly going up and the investors kept on enjoying the opportunity to earn compound return on their original investments.

On the contrary, had Berkshire Hathaway kept on paying dividends every year, the investors would have had to pay personal income tax and the effective rate of return on their investments would have gone down considerably. And, Warren had done this also because the investors did not have better options to reinvest their dividends. Had they invested their dividends in government or corporate bonds earning average 8% returns, they would have had to pay income tax on their income and effective return on their investments would have gone down every year by the rate of income tax.

Beware! Most of the investment analysts do advise investors to invest in shares of companies doing excellent business and hold on to the same for long periods, but they do not tell them at what rate they should buy the shares. However, if we follow Warren Buffett's investment strategy, we would not allow ourselves to be taken for a ride by such investment analysts, as Warren says - rate of return depends on the price paid.

For example, in 1987, shares of the food products and tobacco group Philip Morris were trading at prices between USD 6.07 and USD 10.36 (share split adjusted price) per share. Ten years later, in 1997, the average price of those shares had gone up to USD 44. Had you bought Philip Morris's shares in 1987 at the rate of USD 6.07 and sold the same in 1997, after holding the same for ten years, at the rate of USD 44, your pre-tax compounding rate of return would have been 21.9% approximately. But, had you bought the same shares at the rate of USD 10.36 and sold them at the rate of USD 44, your pre-tax compounding rate of return would have been 15.56% approximately. Thus, your investment of USD 1,00,000 in shares @6.07 per share would have grown in ten years to USD 7,24,497.77 with the annual compounding rate of return of 21.9%. But the same investment of USD 1,00,000 in shares @10.36 per share would have grown to just USD 4,24,693.22 with annual compounding rate of return of 15.56%, i.e., the difference in compound returns for the two purchase prices would have been USD 2,99,804.55. You may easily calculate all this using the free online financial calculator we discussed earlier.

Nine Financial Questions to Pick a Business

It is clear by now that if we want to earn the maximum compound return on our investment, we will have to identify incorporated companies doing excellent business before we determine the right prices for the investment options. To develop the philosophy for identification of an outstanding company, Warren incorporated the philosophies of much-acclaimed American investor Philip Arthur and his partner Charles Thomas Munger (Vice Chairman, Berkshire Hathaway) in the philosophy of his guru Benjamin Graham. And finally, he decided that he would invest only in the companies that had strong economics and whose future income could be estimated properly. For this, Warren uses following questions for evaluation:

Question No. 1: Does the business have an identifiable consumer monopoly?

As we have seen in previous chapter, Warren Buffett had been able to pick many such companies that offered unique products or services and enjoyed monopoly-like status in their segment of the consumer market. Warren has been referring to such companies as 'consumer monopolies', like companies maintaining and operating toll bridges.

In Warren's view, this is a classic form of 'consumer monopoly'. If a consumer wants to cross a river without swimming or using a boat, he may have to pay toll-tax to use a bridge, as toll bridge enjoys near monopoly on crossing the bridge at a specific location. It is the same when a big city is served by a single newspaper. If you have to advertise your product or service in that specific city, you would have to place your advertisement in that very newspaper. Clearly, whether it is a toll bridge at a specific location or an exclusive newspaper in a specific city, consumer monopoly provides them the freedom to fix higher prices for their services.

In fact, Warren Buffett had identified some conceptual tests to confirm presence of 'consumer monopoly' in companies engaged in any specific business. For this, the first question he would ask himself - Had he possessed billions of dollars and had he been capable of employing 50 top managers, could he start the same business and run the same successfully like the concerned company? If the answer was 'No', Warren would assume that the company was protected with some specific kind of consumer monopoly. In Warren's view, the real test for a 'consumer monopoly' company is whether any competitor can, without bothering for its income, harm that company in any way.

For instance, Warren had tried to find out whether it was possible for anybody to compete with 'Wall Street Journal'. And he had figured out that no newspaper, even if it invested billions of dollars, would be able to dent Wall Street Journal's readership. Similarly, he had examined whether he could compete with 'Wrigley' (the world's largest chewing gum manufacturing and marketing company; now a wholly owned subsidiary to Mars Inc.) by launching a company to manufacture tasty chewing gums. Warren had found out that many companies had attempted to compete with 'Wrigley', but most of them had badly failed. And those who could protect their identity also had to be content with their negligible market shares as compared to that of 'Wrigley'. Warren had also made similar assessments for chocolate bar producing company Hershey (now one of the largest chocolate marketing companies in the United States), soft drink company Coca-Cola etc.

For a moment, let's think about Coca-Cola. Just try to imagine all the places where it is sold. You will find Coca-Cola at all street corners, shops of all sizes, restaurants, buildings and public facilities. The popularity of this cold drink compels every shop or restaurant to stock it. Why? Because, non-availability of Coca-Cola might impact their business. Now, try to compete with Coca-Cola. You would need capital base equivalent to two companies of the size of General Motors. You may still not be able to claim that you can compete with Coca-Cola. Only one of its competing companies in the world could grow- that is none other than PepsiCo; because, Coca-Cola has a secret formula to make the cold drink.

Yes, Warren had found out after research that consumer monopoly companies, benefiting from their huge cash flow, are usually almost debt-free. That is the reason such companies are able to launch new enterprises or increase their stakes by buying back their own shares. Not only that, such companies generally manufacture products that require low level of technology and hence, they do not need to set up high-technology plants. As their products face almost negligible competition in the market, they are able to use their manufacturing plants for longer periods. Being free from competition, these companies do not have to incur regular expenses on upgrading their plants. On the other side, let's consider the case of automobile manufacturing companies. They are also price sensitive like commodity products. That is the reason that even to launch just a new car with a fresh design in the market they have to spend billions of dollars on upgrading old machinery and setting up new production facility. And, cars or other motor vehicles are the products that need constant modifications to keep themselves relevant in the cut-throat competition of the market. To do that, motor vehicle companies have to keep making heavy investments in their production facilities on regular basis.

Question No. 2: Are the earnings of the company strong and showing an upward trend?

A company may be enjoying consumer monopoly status but is its top management capable of constantly taking its earnings to higher levels? Yes, just like Warren, we also would have to attentively go through balance sheets of such companies and examine their figures for per share income. For this, Warren used to study at least ten years' balance sheets of the concerned company and make a table of its per share income figures. If the earnings were strong and showed an upward trend, Warren would infer that the top management was able to convert the favourable consumer monopoly status of the company into real shareholders' value.

Question No. 3: What is the long-term debt position of the company? Is it conservatively financed?

Warren likes the companies that hesitate to avail heavy long-term loans. If the company enjoys consumer monopoly, it is definite that its cash flow would be quite good and it would not even need to impose the burden of a long-term loan upon itself. Wrigley and International Flavors & Fragrances are counted among Warren's favourite companies because their books generally do not show any long-term debt and if at all such debts are there, they are negligible. Warren's highly profitable companies like Coca-Cola and Gillette do not allow the load of long-term loans in their books to go beyond their 'current net income'.

However, even excellent companies enjoying consumer monopoly sometimes incur long-term debt to acquire another company; for instance, Capital Cities had availed a long-term loan amounting to more than double of its current net income for acquiring American television and radio network American Broadcasting Corporation (ABC) Group. In such a case, Warren would just check whether the company acquired was a consumer monopoly.

If 'Yes', it was ok else, something was wrong.

In this regard, Warren has clear opinion that if a consumer monopoly company avails a loan to acquire another consumer monopoly company, heavy cash flows of the two together negate the impact of the debt. On the contrary, if a consumer monopoly company incurs debt for acquiring a commodity company, it would definitely impact its profitability even if its cash flow is able to withstand the burden of debt. The third situation is the most dangerous where a commodity company incurs debt to acquire a similar company just for the expansion of its market, as it does not have a definite cash flow for the same.

Question No 4: Does the business consistently earn a high rate of return on shareholders' equity?

Warren Buffett has been investing in only those companies that are capable of consistently earning a high rate of return on equity, as such companies could generate wealth for their shareholders.

Here, equity refers to shareholders' equity. In fact, the shareholders' equity represents the amount left after adjusting total liabilities against total assets. In other words, total of the capital investments made by the shareholders in a business is the shareholders' equity in total assets.

For example, to buy a house for Rs 60 lakh, you invest Rs 15 lakh out of your savings and avail a mortgage loan of Rs 45 lakh from a bank, your i.e., shareholder's equity would be Rs 15 lakh (Rs 60 lakh - Rs 45 lakh) in the total asset of Rs 1 crore. Now, if you rent out this house, the amount left after making payments towards maintenance expenses, equated monthly instalments and house tax would be shareholders' equity. Suppose you rent out the house at Rs 25000 per month, i.e. Rs 3 lakh per year and your total expenses amounts to Rs 2.50 lakh (maintenance expenses of Rs 6000, EMI payments Rs 2.40 lakh and house tax Rs 4000), you are left with Rs 50000 only. Thus, your (the shareholder's)net earningsare Rs 50000 per year (approximately 3.33%) on your capital investment or equity of Rs 15 lakh. In other words, your house (business) earned return on equity at the rate of 3.33% for you (its shareholders).

Similarly, if you own a corporate/company having total assets of Rs 1 crore and the company has a total liability of Rs 40 lakh, it means that you have made a capital investment of Rs 60 lakh in the company and the same represents shareholders' equity in the company. If the company makes a net profit of Rs

19.80 lakh after tax, it means it has earned return on equity at the rate of 33% for you (its shareholders).

In this situation, if Indian companies were collectively earning 12% return on equity, your company would be referred to as 'above average'. And the companies earning less than 12% return on equity would be called 'below average'. Clearly, you would like to invest in companies earning above average return on equity, as they only are able to grow your investment faster i.e., make you rich quicker.

However, Warren Buffett has been treating only those companies as the best, which were able to earn average 15 per cent return on equity at least for the last 10 years; in other words, Warren had invested his precious capital only in the companies that were capable of definitely earning above average return on equity. Yes, when Warren started buying shares in General Food Corporation, its average return on equity was 16 per cent. Similarly, when he started buying shares in Coca-Cola, it was earning 33 per cent return on equity and its average earning was around 25 per cent for the last 5 years. 'Hershey' (chocolate) was one of Warren's favourite companies as its average return on equity for the last ten years was 16.7 per cent. Similarly, when Warren started buying shares in Philip Morris, it was earning 30.5 per cent average return on equity for the last ten years. Also, when Warren acquired a major shareholding in Capital Cities, it was earning 18 per cent return on equity. And, Service Master Global Holdings and Gannett Corporation were earning 40 per cent and 25 per cent returns on equity respectively when Warren had acquired their shares.

Question No 5: Does the business get to retain its earnings?

Warren Buffett believes that the companies that, instead of paying dividends at high rates, are able to retain their net profits to invest the same in more profitable ventures provide their shareholders opportunities to earn compound return through value addition to their original shares. Warren has done the same in his controlling company Berkshire Hathaway. However, he also agrees that all companies that retain their profits are not able to do the same. Hence, we should look into the history of such companies thoroughly.

Question No 6: How much does the business spend on maintaining current operations?

Earning profit, retaining the profit and not spending the retained profit on maintenance of current operations are three different matters. Warren Buffett makes a thorough analysis of these three figures before investing in a company because, if the company is reinvesting surplus retained income into maintaining current operations, there is little money left over to invest in other profitable ventures and to increase the shareholders' fortune.

Suppose a company is making net profit of Rs 1 crore every year. Instead of making dividend payment to its shareholders, it retains the profit; however, it has to spend Rs 2 crore every alternate year on replacing its plant and equipment to maintain its operations. It is hence clear that the net profit of the company is in fact zero. Yes, Warren considers only those business operations to be excellent that have to incur no expenses out of their profits towards replacement of their plant or machinery.

In fact, when Warren Buffett managed night classes at College of Business Administration of Nebraska Omaha University in his hometown Omaha on the subject of investments, he would deliver lectures on capital requirements of companies and their impacts. He would quote examples of AT&T and Thomson Publishing in this regard. Warren would demonstrate that AT&T was a bad investment for its shareholders before its disintegration. Though it was earning good income, it had to arrange funds even more than its income to meet its capital requirements like research & development and infrastructure. AT&T used to issue fresh shares or bonds to finance its expansion. On the contrary, companies like Thomson Publishing were publishing many newspapers in cities having single newspaper and making good money for their shareholders. This was possible for such a company as once its basic infrastructure related to printing press was ready, its capital requirements were minimal and it did not need to use shareholders' money for the same. Hence, such companies used to have a lot of cash to acquire new newspapers and increase shareholders' fortune.

This way, Warren would try to impress upon that while one business was able to achieve its value enhancement without much of capital requirements, the other was not able to grow as it required additional capital investments.

American motor vehicle company General Motors may also be quoted as a reference for the same. Between the start of 1985 and the end of 1995, General Motors had earned an average of USD 17.92 per share and had paid an average dividend of USD 20.60 per share. However, during the same period, the company had to spend total of USD 102.34 per share towards capital requirements involving maintenance, upgradation and expansion of the business. Thus, during those ten years, General Motors had to arrange USD 2.68 per share (20.60 - 17.92) towards payment of dividend more than its income and USD 102.34 per share towards its capital requirements.

Thus, the question naturally arises that how could General Motors arrange such a huge amount? Of course, records reveal that during that period, the company had added around USD 33 billion to its debts i.e., the company had taken an additional debt load of USD 43.70 per share. It is clear that the company had not serviced its requirements out of loans only. During that period, the company had issued 132 million fresh shares out of its common stock. This had resulted in a decline of USD 34.29 in the book value/net worth of each share of General Motors during the period. Its book value per share had gradually declined from USD 45.99 in 1985 to just USD 11.70 in 1995.

But surprisingly, the market value of shares of General Motors did not go down. This was trading at USD 40 per share in the beginning of 1985 and it was floating at the same level even after ten years. This meant that even after ten years of business activities, General Motors did not add any value to shareholders' capital as it had gobbled up primary shareholders' capital by adding debt burden of USD 33 billion and issuing 132 million fresh shares to meet its capital requirements; what did the primary shareholders get on their investments? Just a dividend of USD 20.60 per share! If we calculate its pre-tax compound return, it would be around 5.8 per cent. Now, if we adjust tax and inflation against the same, we may find that the invested capital actually lost its real value during those ten years.

And all this happened because the capital requirements of motor vehicle companies are actually so massive. As designs of cars and trucks kept changing, General Motors had to constantly keep its manufacturing plants upgraded as per new requirements. And as its capital requirements were more than its income, it had to take in extra load of debts and also issue fresh shares to collect additional funds. Thus, General Motors had badly failed in adding any value to the shareholders capital just to keep itself in business.

This was the reason that Warren Buffett never invested in companies like General Motors i.e., motor vehicles businesses that required spending shareholders money to keep themselves operational. Clearly, we should also keep away from investing in businesses that constantly require capital investments in their basic infrastructure and research and development; companies involved in such businesses, irrespective of the expertise of their management, are never able to provide their shareholders opportunities for compound return on their capital investments.

Question No 7: Is the company in a position to reinvest retained earnings in profitable options?

In the course of picking excellent businesses, Warren Buffett has always been probing whether the related company is in a position to reinvest retained earnings in profitable options. Keep in mind that Warren's fundamental investment philosophy is - investment with the perspective of business i.e., investment that provides an opportunity to earn more than average return on capital. Earning more than average refers to options that provide opportunities to earn more than bank or government bonds without any risk.

Suppose you save Rs 10000 every year and keep the same in your cupboard. After ten years, you would have a total of Rs 100,000. Had you deposited the same amount in a recurring deposit account of a bank earning interest at the rate of 5 per cent, the amount would have grown to Rs 1,32,067 at the end of tenth year. Had you invested the same amount, like Warren, in investment options earning compound return of 23 per cent, the amount would have grown to Rs 370,388 at the end of 10th year. And, had you saved the same amount for 20 years with the same rate of return, your savings of Rs 200,000 could have grown to Rs 3,306,059. That means, investment made with Warren's skill could turn Rs 100,000 to Rs 370,388 in ten years, thus earning an extra amount of Rs 270,388 on your actual investment; and in the next ten years, your additional investment of Rs 100,000 could provide you a great opportunity to earn Rs 2,835,671 in the next ten years. This only is Warren's magic of compound interest, and only a company that is able to reinvest its earnings in more profitable ventures to make such magical returns on your long-term investment is an 'excellent business' in Warren's view.

Of course, Warren has done just the same thing in his controlling company Berkshire Hathaway. He did not make dividend payments every year to his investors; instead, he invested the earnings in more profitable ventures and provided an opportunity to his investors to earn compound return much above an average of 23 per cent on their shareholdings. It may be noted that Warren had applied his magical investment philosophy even in the companies where he has acquired minority stakes. Take for example Capital Cities. What did it do before its merger with Disney? Capital Cities had retained the earnings from its high-cash-flow cable TV business and utilised the same to acquire ABC Group's TV network that itself was a high-cash-flow business. In other words, Capital Cities had reinvested its shareholders retained earnings in more profitable options. ABC Group was a kind of consumer monopoly company as federal laws at that time protected markets of companies involved in TV business and there was no market competition as is prevalent today. As setting up a TV centre required only an initial capital investment and the same could exist for next 40 years, ABC Group was in a position to reinvest retained earnings of its shareholders in more profitable ventures instead of utilising the same for its own capital requirements.

Though TV network business, on account of competition, did not continue to be a very profitable business later, Warren had continued to count the same among 'excellent businesses' for a long time, as the number of main competing companies in any market sector of the United States of America continued to be only three (ABC, CBS and NBC) and they all were able to get their share of advertisements. More or less, the situation in media business continues to be the same even today and this business is more profitable in terms of long-term investment. As the capital requirements of this business is limited, it can fund its market expansion needs with retain earnings of its shareholders and provide them opportunities to earn compound return for a long period.

Question No 8: Is the company free to adjust prices to inflation?

We all know that inflation is a major cause for increase in prices of products and services; however, all businesses are not able to adjust market prices of their products and services to inflation. Now, if we consider a commodity business, we can find that, despite increase in the cost of labour and raw materials, the companies in this sector when faced with higher production, are compelled to lower prices of their products instead of adjusting the same to inflation. It is clear that, in an attempt to sell their products at prices lower than their production costs just to keep themselves in business, they cover their loss with their shareholders' retained earnings. And, when even that is not sufficient to meet their requirements, they increase their debt burden or collect funds by issuing fresh shares. This results in gradual decline in book value/ net worth of the company; it hence finds itself unable to increase value of shareholders' capital investments.

Aviation business also faces similar situations from time to time. All kinds of fixed costs of aviation companies keep growing with inflation. And when they are faced with competition, they are compelled to sell tickets at prices even below their actual costs just to keep themselves in business. It is obvious that they also have to indulge in utilising their shareholders' retained earnings, worsening their debt burden and collecting funds by issuing fresh shares to meet their capital requirements. Thus, they are left with no capital to reinvest in profitable ventures and are not able to add value to their shareholders' capital investments.

Yes, Warren keeps himself away from such businesses that are not in a position to reinvest their shareholders' retained earnings in more profitable ventures, as they are not free to adjust prices of their products to inflation.

Question No 9: Will the value added by retained earnings increase the market value of the company?

Warren's guru Benjamin Graham also, during the last years of his professional life, had said that the capital market consisted of two components. The first was long-term investment centred such that over the long-term, the market price of a company's share would reflect its intrinsic value. The other component was like a gambling house where people would bet on short term fluctuations in market prices.

Graham believed that the gambling house component of the market was dominated by the organisations or people who speculated on the impact of daily news on share prices. At the same time, Graham also maintained that this very gambling house aspect of the market provided the patient investors focused on long-term investments the opportunities to test their skills. For some time, when groups having speculative mentality are dominated by people's fear and greed, market prices also crash in anillogical manner thus providing patient investors to acquire shares of companies at prices even lower than their intrinsic values.

Definitely, Warren also had embraced his guru's this very philosophy in his professional life; he had even made an addition to the same. Warren has always maintained that if a company allocates its capital properly and keeps on improving its book value / net worth consistently, the long-term investment tendency of the market would constantly reflect the same in the market price of its share. The same thing had happened with Warren's own company Berkshire Hathaway. The company had kept on improving its book value by investing shareholders earnings in profitable ventures and the same had been reflected in the market price of its shares. This was the reason that while looking for excellent companies, Warren would definitely investigate whether the value addition by a company through retain earnings was actually getting reflected in its market value.

And, these very nine questions had made Warren Buffett successful in picking excellent companies and finding the opportunities for earning magical compound returns through long-term investments in them.

❑

3

Picking the Right Manager

Sometime in the middle of December 2016, around a month after Donald Trump getting elected as the 45th President of the United States of America on 8 November, when the major stock market index Dow Jones Industrial Average (DJIA) was approaching the figure of 20000, not only the USA but the entire world was immersed in discussions on impending changes in international politics. Very few people at that time would have thought about Warren Buffett as one of the top beneficiaries of the bull run in stock markets. The price of a share of his company Berkshire Hathaway had touched the level of USD 249,711 for the first time on 13 December and after some fluctuations, had reached the level of USD 266,013 on 1 March 2017.

It was some 52 years back, in May 1965, when Warren Buffett had taken over control of Berkshire Hathaway. During that period, the price of a share of Berkshire Hathaway had gone up at the rate of 21 per cent per annum against the average annual return of just 2.075 per cent for Dow Jones Industrial Average (DJIA). Obviously, this performance of Buffett's company had gone beyond even the flight of a mind. Thus, had somebody invested USD 1000 in shares of Berkshire Hathaway in 1964, that investment would have grown to USD 45 million after 52 years. Now the biggest question is - how could Warren Buffettdeliver such an amazing performance? Most of the people would just say that he is the world's greatest investor. There is no doubt in the fact that Warren Buffett has been the greatest and the most successful investor of our time, but this is not a complete answer to the question. The most overlooked point of view in respect of Buffett is that he has been an extraordinarily successful manager also. And, this is also the most useful and inspiring point of view for the leaders of business world.

Yes, Warren Buffett is the only particular individual who has been in command of a large multinational conglomerate like Berkshire Hathaway for the last 52 years. This needs to be given special attention. Perhaps the most talked about chief executive officer in the commercial history of the United States was the one who had run General Motors for 23 years. John D. Rockefeller had managed Standard Oil for 27 years and in recent times, Bill Gates had been chief executive officer of Microsoft for 25 years. However, it is surprising that even though investors around the world try to follow Buffett's investment approach, it may be right to say that his management model has not made any impact on corporate work culture. In this connection, Buffett's old friend and Vice Chairman of Berkley Hathaway Charlie Munger has said in his letter written to shareholders in 2016, "Berkshire system is essential for its success. I am not aware if any other corporate has even half of these elements".

Development of the Skill of Delegating Authority

When Berkshire Hathaway got bigger and bigger and took over control of multiple businesses, Warren Buffett felt the essentiality of 'delegation of authority'. This was required not only for his sanity i.e., his ability to think and behave in a normal and rational manner but also to ensure that the companies were managed competently and managers were happy running them. If there is a single management skill that is uniquely Warren's, it would be his willingness and promptness to 'delegate authority'. In fact, the boldness that Warren has exhibited in delegating unlimited authority to his managers may be a cause of worry for most of the chief executive officers. And this is the biggest reason that made Warren Buffett successful in transforming a regional textile company like Berkshire Hathaway into a giant multinational conglomerate.

Yes, Berkshire Hathaway is a public holding company owning more than 88 companies engaged in different kinds of businesses. Managers vested with complete authority run all these companies. A total of 367,700 employees work in those companies and Warren Buffett, sitting in headquarters located in his hometown Omaha, guides them from the top. In the annual report of Berkshire Hathaway for the year 1999, Warren Buffett had himself given an account of his managerial skills that you may not find anywhere else.

"Berkshire's collection of managers is unusual in several important ways. As one example, a very high percentage of these men and women are independently wealthy, having made fortunes in the businesses that they run. They work neither because they need the money nor because they are contractually obligated to — we have no contracts at Berkshire. Rather, they work long and hard because they love their businesses. And I use the word "their" advisedly, since these managers are truly in charge — there are no show-and-tell presentations in Omaha, no budgets to be approved by headquarters, no dictums issued about capital expenditures. We simply ask our managers to run their companies as if these are the sole asset of their families and will remain so for the next century."

"Charlie (Munger) and I try to behave with our managers just as we attempt to behave with Berkshire's shareholders, treating both groups as we would wish to be treated if our positions were reversed. Though "working" means nothing to me financially, I love doing it at Berkshire for some simple reasons: It gives me a sense of achievement, a freedom to act as I see fit and an opportunity to interact daily with people I like and trust. Why should our managers — accomplished artists at what they do — see things differently?"

"In their relations with Berkshire, our managers often appear to be hewing to President Kennedy's charge, "Ask not what your country can do for you; ask what you can do for your country". Here's a remarkable story from last year: It's about R. C. Willey, Utah's dominant home furnishing business, which Berkshire purchased from Bill Child and his family in 1995. Bill and most of his managers are Mormons, and for this reason R. C. Willey's stores have never operated on Sunday. This is a difficult way to do business: Sunday is the favourite shopping day for many customers. Bill, nonetheless, stuck to his principles -- and while doing so built his business from $250,000 of annual sales in 1954, when he took over, to $342 million in 1999.

"Bill felt that R. C. Willey could operate successfully in markets outside of Utah and in 1997 suggested that we open a store in Boise. I was highly sceptical about taking a no-Sunday policy into a new territory where we would be up against entrenched rivals open seven days a week. Nevertheless, this was Bill's business to run. So, despite my reservations, I told him to follow both his business judgment and his religious convictions.

"Bill then insisted on a truly extraordinary proposition: He would personally buy the land and build the store — for about $9 million as it turned out — and would sell it to us at his cost if it proved to be successful. On the other hand, if sales fell short of his expectations, we could exit the business without paying Bill a cent. This outcome, of course, would leave him with a huge investment in an empty building. I told him that I appreciated his offer but felt that if Berkshire was going to get the upside it should also take the downside. Bill said nothing doing: If there was to be failure because of his religious beliefs, he wanted to take the blow personally."

"The store opened last August and immediately became a huge success. Bill thereupon turned the property over to us — including some extra land that had appreciated significantly — and we wrote him a check for his cost. And get this: Bill refused to take a dime of interest on the capital he had tied up over the two years."

"If a manager has behaved similarly at some other public corporation, I haven't heard about it. You can understand why the opportunity to partner with people like Bill Child causes me to tap dance to work every morning".

Yes, Warren Buffett lost no time in realising that every leader must learn the skill of 'delegation of authority' to run a business and ensure its sustained growth. Beware! It is a natural inclination of a leader to control every minor and major incident connected to his work, venture and business and the people involved. However, any attempt to micro-manage so many jobs, ventures and businesses at the same time is like throwing many balls in air and attempting to prevent them from falling on ground, just like a circus juggling artist giving his performance. In such a case, even a slight loss of attention by the leader may have the risk of everything falling apart. Not only that, when a leader at the top tries to control every activity, his more important tasks in fact get neglected. But, if that leader delegates authority to able managers focusing on specific tasks and oversees and guides the entire business, all the jobs get executed smoothly and he does not lose his focus on more critical jobs.

This was the reason that Warren had picked highly efficient managers / chief executive officers for each of his companies and had also delegated to them all necessary executive authority to allow them to carry out their operational responsibilities related to concerned businesses. Just as Warren has given the example of Utah's home furnishing business, he delegates complete control of his business to every chief executive officer. When Berkshire acquired an American manufacturer of recreational vehicles, cargo trailers, utility trailers, pontoon boats and buses in June 2005, Warren made it clear to its founder and chief executive officer Peter Liegl not to expect to hear from him more than once a year. Not only that, Berkshire in May 2003 acquired American supply chain services company McLane Company from Walmart for USD 1.45 billion. When William Grady Rosier, who had been the president and chief executive officer of McLane since 1995, contacted Warren Buffett over phone for approval of purchase of some company jets, Warren told him, "This is your decision. It is your company to run".

Warren's this quote is quite popular, "We delegate authority almost to the point of abdication". Yes, Warren felt it would be sheer folly on his part to think he could competently manage each and every one of his businesses himself. He has hence delegated complete responsibility to all his managers and chief executive officers with regard to management of their related businesses and also authority to take all decisions for their operations. Yes, this is boldness almost to the point of abdication. However, Warren has also formulated some rules for delegation of authority: they are as follows:

Every business culture is unique: Warren Buffett was well aware that every business - small or large - has its own unique work culture. Workers and managers connected to every business have their own highly specialised skills that allow them to accomplish their tasks efficiently. Warren had quickly learnt that he could not perform jobs like those highly skilled managers and hence, he allowed those specialised workers only to perform their tasks without any interference. Warren also realised that the only responsibility he had as a management leader was to inspire his employees to attain their greatness. Warren has always held himself in the role of a cheerleader and never allowed himself to become a slave driver. He believes that his employees are the experts and they should be allowed to perform jobs in which they have expertise. This only would ensure utilisation of full potential of the workers in the interest of the company. And then only, it would be possible to protect the personal interest of the employees.

Competent managers like to do their business as their own: Warren Buffetthad quickly discovered the mystery of management psychology that most of the business-owners fail to understand. Warren felt that managers who were really competent liked to be left alone to run their business and they were unable to tolerate any interference in their work. They liked to manage their business the way they deem proper. And if they were allowed to consider their business as their own, they did wonders. Warren did the same thing. After completing the process of selection, he has been maintaining 100 per cent confidence in his managers and encouraging them to manage their 'own' business in their 'own' way. He has been taking pride in standing behind them in all instances of their minor and major mistakes. As a result, the managers/ chief executive officers of associate companies of Berkshire work hard like owners and ensure the best performance for their 'own' businesses. For them, it is a matter of pride.

Competence, hard work and passion must come with integrity: Before delegating full authority to his managers, Warren Buffett has been making sure that besides being competent, hardworking and passionate, they also have a great deal of integrity. Warren has sensed that a manager who is hardworking, passionate and expert in his business-related jobs but lacks integrity may use all his expertise to rob the company blind. Hence, Warren pays maximum attention to integrity in his managers - though rest all the qualities are of course required to run the business efficiently.

It is worth noting that, during the acquisition of Nebraska Furniture Mart, he had given maximum importance to 'Mrs. B' and allowed her only to run the business for her entire life. Mrs. B's motto was 'sell cheap and tell the truth'. And, Warren was just crazy about that line.

Initial Success of Investor Buffett

In 1956, Warren Buffett's guru Benjamin Graham had handed over the reins of his company 'Graham-Newman Corporation' to his partner Jerry Newman and like a celebrity, started living a luxurious retired life in Beverly Hills (a city in California, surrounded by Los Angeles and West Hollywood)while also teaching at California University, Los Angeles. During 21 years (1936 to 1956) of his teaching at Columbia University, Graham had firmly established his partnership investment concern

'Graham-Newman Corporation' in the world's largest capital market 'Wall Street' (New York) and earned an average income of 17 per cent that was more than 14 per cent growth of 'Standard & Poor's 500' index. This did not include the earnings on shares of Government Employees Insurance Company (GEICO), the best investment of Graham-Newman Corporation, though the same was available for distribution to its shareholders. The shareholders, who had held on to the shares of GEICO, were earning almost double in comparison to the S&P 500 index.

However, after completing his studies at Columbia University in 1950, Warren Buffett was regularly making investments at his own level silently and while working with 'Graham-Newman Corporation', had seen his personal investment capital jump from USD 9800 to USD 140,000 in 1956. With enough capital of his own, he was getting impatient to move back to his hometown Omaha. Another major reason was Benjamin Graham's relocation to Beverley Hills, as after that, Buffett was not enjoying working under Jerry Newman's uninspiring leadership.

Hence, during the spring of 1956, Warren Buffett and his wife Susan had rented a house a little away from his grandfather's grocery store 'Buffett Grocery' in Omaha. This time, Buffett had no plans to work for his father's brokerage firm or for anybody else. On the very day when he arrived Omaha from New York on 1 May, he arranged an informal meeting for his family members and friends. In the meeting, seven limited partners - Buffett's sister Doris and her husband, aunt Elis, Doc Thomson, his old hostel roommate Chuck Peterson and his mother and his attorney Dan Monen - together pooled USD 1,05,000. Warren Buffett himself contributed only USD 100 as a general partner. This was a very nominal amount but this time, Buffett was going to use this investment not for his father or guru Benjamin Graham but for his own proposed partnership firm Buffett Associates Ltd.

This was the time when medical practitioner Homer Dose, an old investor of Graham-Newman Corporation, had asked Benjamin Graham, "Who is now going to carry forward your 'intellectual legacy?" Graham had responded, "Warren Buffett".

And when Homer Dose was on his trip to the West in his car for his summer vacation, he had made a stop-over at Omaha for sometime. After only a short conversation with Warren Buffett, Dose had announced his decision to invest USD 1,20,000 in Buffett's partnership firm and had continued with his journey.

Thus, Buffett started managing three small partnership firms from his bedroom and he could also visualise great potentials for the future of his family partnership. A few months later, Buffett returned to New York to participate in the last meeting of the shareholders of Graham-Newman Corporation. There, he mentioned to Benjamin Graham's another follower Ed Anderson that he was contemplating launching a partnership firm like 'Graham-Newman' with a minimum investment of USD 50000. After the shareholders of Graham-Newman Corporation had cast their formal votes at the end of their activities, the chief of Manhattan located brokerage firm commented that Graham had made a big mistake by failing in developing talents. He further elaborated that Graham-Newman could have carried on with its operations further only because he had an extraordinary lad named Warren Buffett. Who would like to drive with him now?

In the beginning of 1957, Warren Buffett was managing an investment fund of USD 300,000 of some of his relatives and friends. Now, Buffett needed large capital to do something different from other anonymous stock pickers in Omaha. But what else did Buffett have, other than demonstrating self-confidence in his abilities, to win the trust of large investors? Buffett did not have any track record of working as an independent investment operator. He had nothing, on paper, to indicate that he was worthy of people's trust. Still, Warren did not want mere discretion over people's money; he wanted absolute control over it. He did not want anybody to raise any question on his stock investment related decisions; he was not ready to have any boss as at 'Graham-Newman'.

However, by now, Buffett was quite familiar with all kinds of information related to almost every share of stock and debt security/bond. He was regularly reading 'Wall Street Journal' and other financial newspapers and magazines besides Moody's Manual and its other books and financial reports, and in the process, was building the entire mental portrait of the Wall Street day by day. He had started to understand every movement in the stock market and the most important point was that he believed in his own analysis only and did not consider the analysis of any of the financial analysts of Wall Street trustworthy. In the situation, what more than Buffett's self-confidence and clear frame of mind could have won people's confidence? And, did Buffett really need anything else but these very features defining his character?

In the summer of 1957, he got a call from Edwin Davis, a prominent Omaha urologist. As Buffett had never met him earlier, he was a bit surprised also. But Davis had very soon made it clear that his investment consultant in New York had suggested Buffett's name. In fact, that consultant had come in contact with Buffett when the latter was working for Graham-Newman. Somebody had informed that consultant that Buffett was working in Omaha and he was looking for some big investment. That is how he had referred Buffett to Davis. Though Davis was not feeling comfortable to trust a novice like Buffett, he had made up his mind to talk to Buffett directly.

When Buffett reached Davis's home on the appointed Sunday, he found that Davis had gathered his entire family there. That was a great moment of Buffett's professional life, not only because he could raise large capital from Dr Davis but also because it could open door for him to other big investors. However, Davis family was surprised that Buffett had not told them anything that could make them happy. On the contrary, Buffett had made it clear that he would not reveal to them where their money was going to be invested. Not only that, Buffett had told that he would come back to them with results of their investments only at the end of year, on 31 December, when they would be free to add more investments or withdraw their capital. Otherwise, the invested capital would be under his complete control. Buffett, in his presentation, was just repeating the business principles of his guru Benjamin Graham. He was putting forward his points quite patiently but his intention was quite clear. He was badly in need of Davis family's capital but he wanted the same at his own terms.

Buffett had placed the terms of business in front of Davis family. Davis family would get a percentage of total profit in the capacity of a limited partner and out of the rest, 75 per cent would go to Davis family and 25 per cent to Buffett. And if the results were average or worse, Buffett would get nothing - no salary, no fee, no expenses. Thus, Buffett had convinced Davis family that he was not asking them to gamble alone; Buffett himself also was taking risk. Buffett had left after his presentation. Davis family deliberated on the matter after that. Though Buffett's terms were crystal clear, majority of the family members were not finding any solid reason to leave their capital in the hands of Buffett and silently wait for the year to end. However, Dr Davis's wife Dorothy unilaterally declared that she had liked everything about young Buffett, and finally, Dr Edwin Davis decided to put up USD 100,000.

Thus, by the end of 1957, Warren Buffett was running five small partnerships, totalling in the range of USD 500,000. His investment portfolio had gained 10 per cent during the first year whereas Dow Jones Industrial Average (DJIA) had got stuck at 8 per cent.

This was the time when Susan was to give birth to their third child. Buffett was quite optimistic about his future based on his first year's income, and as a long-term investment, bought a five-bedroom house on Farnam Street in anupper-middle class suburban neigh bourhood in Omaha for USD 31,500. The master bedroom had now been converted into Buffett's office and he would operate all his companies from there only.

In 1958, Buffett's investment portfolio had gained 41 per cent against 39 per cent return of DJIA. Thus, the original partnership capital had doubled by the end of third year. Simultaneously, Buffett was bringing new investors into his fold and he had also increased the minimum investment limit to join the partnership to USD 50,000. Buffett had made a lot of effort to buy 10 per cent shares of stock of National American Fire Insurance, an obscure insurance company in Omaha, during its buy-back offer; this had given him the opportunity to make his first grand income of USD 100,000.

Buffett's next target was Sanborn Map Company, developer and publisher of maps for American towns and cities, whose once-lucrative business had been ruined by depression. Sanborn Maps had made lot of investments during its good times and its book value was around USD 65. But the same had come down to USD 45 on account of map business not doing well. As per the investment lesson learnt from Graham, this was a golden opportunity as today or tomorrow, the book value was in any case going to be reflected in its market price. Hence, Buffett had continued buying Sanborn shares during 1958 and 1959. As the original directors of Sanborn were holding just 400 shares and the falling price of 105,000 shares issued in the market did not impact them anyway, they were not showing any interest in lifting their price. Not only that, sitting on a huge investment portfolio, the company directors had paid dividends on only five occasions during the last eight years, though they had not affected any reduction in their own fees. In the circumstances, Graham had managed, on the strength of his shareholding, to take a position among the board of directors and had started putting pressure on the management for disclosure of the real value of the investment portfolio. Eventually in 1960, Sanborn management had agreed to utilise its huge investment portfolio and bring out a buy-back offer; and thus, Buffett had got the opportunity for 50% return on his investment. In fact, Buffett had invested 35% of all the assets of his investors in shares of Sanborn Maps only. Obviously, Buffett had got a chance to reap the returns on the risk he had taken.

Buffett understood the importance of the 'right manager'

Though Buffett had just been successful in winning the trust of a group of ten practitioners and attracting a total investment capital of USD 1,00,000 (USD 10000 per practitioner), he was yet to emerge as a large investment operator. Perhaps that was the reason that, after two very successful ventures, he decided next year to take the biggest risk till date and staked USD 1 million on Dempster Mill Manufacturing Company (Beatrice, Nebraska).

Located in Beatrice, Nebraska, 90-miles south of Omaha, Dempster Mill Manufacturing Company was an 80-year-old manufacturer of windmills and farm equipment. Though Dempster was sick due to static sales and negligible profitability of windmills, Buffett found the market price of its shares quite attractive. In 1961, he used 20% of the capital of his investors to acquire a controlling holding of 70% in Dempster and appoint himself as chairman of the company. Generally, investors try to keep themselves away from the hassle of management, but Buffett was marching ahead on an unknown path of future like a prophet.

Buffett convinced his trusted attorney and investor friend Dan Monen also to join the board of directors. Every month, Buffett, along with Monen, would make a 90-miles trip in his car to dusty town of Beatrice but he was still unable to have a grip on Dempster. The company required radical changes but they were beyond Buffett's expertise. He would instruct his managers every month to bring down overhead expenses and reduce inventory. They would even nod their heads in agreement. Buffett would return to Omaha and next time, Buffett would still find the problems existing as before. All this made Buffett to put the company on sale.

On the other side, Buffett had already invested partnership capital in, besides Dempster, 40 other shares of stocks. Though Dempster's issue was yet to be resolved, other investments brought in unprecedented returns for Buffett. In the first five years of his business, he was able to consistently beat Dow Jones Industrial Index (DJIA). (See table)

Buffett Versus Dow Jones

Year	Annual gain (%) for Buffett's Partners	Annual Return rate (%) of Dow Jones Industrial Average Index
1957	+10.4	-8.4
1958	+40.9	+38.5
1959	+25.9	+19.9
1960	+22.8	-6.3
1961	+45.9	+22.2
5-years' cumulative gain	**251.0**	**74.3**

Source: Buffett: The Making of An American Capitalist (Roger Lowenstein/Random House/1985)

The above table 'Buffett versus Dow Jones' clearly indicates that while Dow Jones (DJIA) was up only three quarters during five years from 1957 to 1961, Buffett's portfolios two and half times. Word of Buffett's amazing success spread like wildfire among the investors in his hometown Omaha. People would descend on him and ask for tips whenever he visited his favourite Ross's steak House or Omaha Country Club. But Buffett wanted to use his skills only for himself. Hence, he would somehow manage, keeping his natural decency intact, to avoid them with his witting answers. He was possessive about stocks, like an artist with an unfinished canvas. He enjoyed narrating stories of his coups to others, but only when they were wrapped up.

Buffett's passion outside his work was the game of bridge. He had a regular game, the members of which included the nobility of the town like ad executive, Buick (car) dealer, judge, life insurance agent, mortgage service provider and railway attorney. Buffett would show up with six packs of Pepsi-Cola and entertain the guys with a stream of jokes and stories. But, he would not talk about the money he was making, as he did not want to. He played quite intensely as if taking decisions on stocks and bonds. He hated to lose and he would play for high stakes only when he thought his team had an edge. Buffett was also unique as he would just stare at the cards and calculate the odds like a machine.

And, Buffett was using this very talent to win over large investors in New York and collect six-figure cheques. For this, he was feeding off Benjamin Graham's network. He met Marshal Weinberg, a broker and fellow Graham alumnus, at 'New School', a private research university located in New York. He and Weinberg soon became friends and Weinberg and his brothers invested USD 100,000 in Buffett's partnership. Similarly, another broker friend Henry Brandt also invested and steered his clients to Buffett. Laurence Tisch, tipped off by Howard Newman, his former colleague at Graham-Newman, had invested USD 100,000.

Around that very time in New York, Buffett met David Strassler whose family was in the business of fixing distressed companies. Strassler had later flown to Omaha to look into acquiring Dempster. Being educated at Harvard Business School and Massachusetts Institute of Technology (MIT), Strassler was very proud of his merit. Buffett had come to the airport to pick him up. When Buffett, after driving a bit, started asking him questions about a company in which his family had a majority stake, he felt quite surprised. In fact, Buffett was asking him about Billings & Spencer that made metal forging products and only about 2% of it was public. But Buffett knew everything about the company. And Strassler was totally cold when Buffett started asking him questions about the balance sheet of the company. He was so impressed by Buffett that he had immediately decided to invest in his partnership.

By 1962, Buffett's partnership companies had a total capital of around USD 7.2 million that was bigger than that of Graham-Newman Corporation. Of that total, USD 1 million belonged to Buffett. Though Buffett's partnership was still quite small compared to large investment firms of Wall Street, it was not unproven. As such, Buffett was still unknown to the common people but he was no longer obscure among investors. Starting with just seven core investors, Buffett had, within just six year, grown the figure to 90 that included groups from California to Vermont. Hence, Buffett merged all his partnerships to form a new company 'Buffett Partnership Limited' and enhanced the limit of minimum investment to USD 100,000. His business had now outgrown his bedroom and hence, he moved his office to Kiewit Plaza, a fourteen-storey tower on Farnam Street near his house.

In the meantime, Buffett developed friendship with Charlie Munger, six years his senior. Having grown up in Omaha, Munger was the son of a lawyer and grandson of a judge. After completing his graduation at Harvard Law School, he had started practising in Los Angeles. In 1959, when Munger returned to Omaha to close out his father's practice, Edwin Davis's son, one of Buffett's investors, was struck by his likeness to Munger and invited the two of them to lunch at Omaha Club with the aim of introducing them to each other. And they soon became close friends. This friendship evolved further when Buffett went to California the same year on vacation with his wife and children. Munger was unimpressive physically but Buffett was quite impressed by his intellect and self-confidence. Buffett advised Munger to focus on his practice but Buffett was quite surprised when Munger had termed his practice as 'waste of his talent and time'.

In fact, like Buffett, Munger also had a considerable passion to get rich - not because he wanted Ferraris - he desperately wanted to be financially independent. This was the reason that even though he had started a new law firm 'Munger, Tolles & Hills'after returning from Harvard, he barely practised there. In 1962, when Buffett moved his office to Kiewit Plaza, Munger was running his own investment partnership. In the meantime, Buffett had started to consider Munger more a consultant than his friend. The same year in spring, Buffett went to Los Angeles to meet Munger only to discuss Dempster issue. Munger was no Benjamin Graham disciple. Munger advised Buffett to sell

Dempster even at a loss, as he felt it was quite difficult to put things right for a troubled company.

But Munger knew a fellow named Harry Bottle who could be a suitable manager for Dempster. Buffett interviewed Bottle in Los Angeles and Bottle was on the job in Beatrice (Nebraska) six days later. Strictly following Buffett's directions, Bottle cut overheads, closed many loss-making plants and brought the inventory to the lowest level. That year-end, Buffett, in the letter to his partners, had referred to Bottle as the man of the year. One year later, when Dempster was quite trimmer and more profitable and its USD 2 million worth of securities were making its financial condition strong, Buffett sold it on a profit of USD 2.3 million. Thus, Buffett was able to triple his investment within three years.

Buffett could achieve this feat because he had bought Dempster at a very low price compared to its book value. Instead of selling the same in panic, he patiently held on to it and picked the 'right manager' like Harry Bottle for its turnaround.

This incident had made Buffett understand the importance of picking the 'right manager' for a company to succeed. Buffett later also felt that the 'right manager' should be retained as long as possible, as like changes in marital relationships, changes in management also are troublesome, time-taking and unpredictable.

Skill of Picking the 'Leader' in a Crowd

This quote from Warren Buffett is quite interesting:

"Would you rather be the world's greatest lover, but have everyone think you're the world's worst lover? Or would you rather be the world's worst lover but have everyone think you're the world's greatest lover?"

Buffett has thus developed his own principle - everybody has either inner scorecard or outer scorecard; he is either true to himself or becomes the one that he feels the world wants him to be. A true leader follows his own drumbeats while bureaucracy submits to others' perceived desires.

Yes, it is quite difficult to stand alone when popular public opinion is against you. However, this very talent of Warren Buffett made him so rich. He buys shares of stocks when everybody else is fearful. He always lives his life against herd behaviour. He has always been free from misconceptions and beliefs and has remained an independent thinker and that is the reason he never faced defeat and was always a winner. In fact, independent thinkers like Buffett never fall prey to misconceptions and beliefs. They are masters of their own destiny. The world-famous quote of Swami Vivekananda that 'You are the maker of your own destiny' also refers to the same.

What is the difference between a loser and a winner mentality? Psychologists believe the two differ in 'locus of control' only. If your locus of control is internal, you blame yourself for anything going wrong. You believe that you are in charge of your fate and can control your results. And in such a mental state, you blame your actions only for your failures. On the contrary, when the 'locus of control' is external, you blame others only, not yourself, for anything going wrong.

In fact, Warren Buffett thinking was highly impacted by his father Howard Homan Buffett. It was on 13 August 1931, just two weeks shy of Warren's first birthday, when his father returned from work with news that his bank had closed. It was the defining, faith-shattering scene of the Great Depression. His job as a securities salesman in Union State Bank was gone. Very soon, his savings also were exhausted. Though Howard's father Ernest had his own grocery store, he gave his son little time to pay for his grocery bills – a bitter pill, as he had inherited the Buffett's disdain for borrowing – "Save your credit, for that is better than money". He sensed bleak prospects, but soon he had announced opening of 'Buffett, Sklenicka & Co.' with an office in Union State Bank building on Farnam Street. This was the same street in Omaha where Warren Buffett was to later stay and work.

It is worth mentioning here that Warren Buffett's grandfather Ernest had married a girl of his own choice against the wishes of his elder brother and that had resulted in acrimony on both sides and they were not on talking terms. As a result, Ernest had to leave his family grocery store located at Omaha city centre. But Ernest wanted to take his family expertise forward and hence in 1915, he established a grocery store in the name of 'Buffett & Sons' in the west side of the town. This was Ernest's clever step as Omaha was expanding in the west. Sensing the opportunity in the suburbs, Ernest started the business with credit facilities and home delivery. Very soon, chefs of rich families started placing orders with Buffett & Sons over phone. Business picked up rapidly. Ernest would extract work from his workers for 11-hours shift quite brutally.

However, Howard Buffett did not have any interest in becoming the third-generation grocery store operator. He also had independent thinking like his father but had a comparatively soft nature - not used to scolding or threatening anybody. Howard worked for sometime for a company engaged in laying gas pipelines, but he was in fact interested in doing something intellectual. He had been editor of 'Daily Nebraskan' in Nebraska University (Lincoln) and longed to have a professional life in journalism. This was the time when Leila Stahl also had joined the university. Raised in West Point (Nebraska) 82-miles west of Omaha, Leila had to work for her father's weekly newspaper for three years after she finished her high school at the age of 16, to arrange funds for her fee for admission into a university. She had contacted Howard asking for a job in 'Daily Nebraskan'. Leila was beautiful. Howard hired her and also immediately asked her for a date. The attraction was there on both sides. When his graduation neared, Howard asked for her hand. Her father John Stahl gave his blessings hoping that Leila would finish her college. A day after Christmas in 1925, when West Point was freezing with temperature 10 degrees below zero, marriage of Leila and Howard was solemnised. They travelled to Omaha on bus instead of going on honeymoon.

Like a dream come true, Howard had already been offered a newspaper job, but his father's friend had also kept a $25-a-week job for him in an insurance company. Howard abandoned his dream of journalism and deferred to his father who had paid his university expenses. This was the need of the time. The couple started their life in a two-bedroom wooden bungalow with a coal furnace, on Baker Avenue, Omaha. For Leila who was raised by an invalid mother, this was a tough beginning. She was not ready to be a homemaker. Howard used his car while Leila would use public transport for her part-time secretarial or printing jobs and many a times, would make more in a week than Howard did. Leila had to attend to a load of housework after returning from work. Around that time, Leila had to go through an eye operation and she was getting regular headaches. When Leila delivered her first child Doris in 1928, she was having 105 degrees fever. And two years later, Leila delivered her second child Warren Edward Buffett on 30 August 1930 in humid summer, with cloudbursts breaking in the 89-degree heat.

By the time Warren began school, his father's fortunes were rapidly improving. When Warren turned six, Buffett family moved to a brick-house on suburban 53-North Street. The bad times in Buffett home were not discussed anymore; they were banished forever. The same year, when Howard took his family on summer vacation to Okoboji (a town located on east side of West Okoboji lake of North-West Iowa), six-year old Warren had tested his first endeavour. He bought a six-pack of Cokes for 25 cents and sold the same to tourists around the lake for 5 cents each, thus making a profit of 5 cents. Back in Omaha, Warren would buy soda pop from his grandfather's store and sell the same door-to-door on summer nights while other children played in the street. Yes, Warren developed his passion for moneymaking then itself. He was not thinking about getting pocket money but about advancing towards his great aspiration.

When Warren was seven, he was hospitalised with a mysterious fever. Doctors removed his appendix, but he still remained so ill that the doctors feared he would die. Even when his father offered him his favourite noodle soup, Warren refused to eat. But left alone, he picked a pencil and filled a page with numbers. These, he told his nurse, represented his future capital. Warren said cheerfully, "I do not have much money now, but someday I will and I will have my picture in newspapers". Purportedly, even in his death throes, Warren was seeking succour not in soup but in dreams of money. It is said that after this incident, Howard Buffett got determined not to let Warren experience the hardships he had gone through. He also resolved that he would not follow his father Ernest and demean his son After that, Howard unfailingly expressed confidence in Warren and supported him in whatever he did. As Warren could never develop close relations with his irritable mother, his universe revolved around his father.

Six-feet tall Howard Buffett with his imposing personality towered over the family, physically and in other respects. He worked hard for supporting his family, owning not only his brokerage firm but also the South Omaha Feed Co. But he was quite excited about money. His passions were religion and politics. He was a self-consciously moral man and had the courage to express his beliefs. Overall, Howard Buffett was extremely conservative. He would remind his children of their duty not only to God but also to community. He was true to his words. He did not ever drink or smoke. When a close investor's securities performed badly, he felt bad enough to repurchase them for his own account. He was elected four times to the US House of Representatives as Republican candidate, but he always indulged in ethical politics. He would even tell Warren always that he himself, not the world, was in control of his life; hence he only would decide how he wanted to lead his life.

But it is not simple to keep 'locus of control' always internal. In that situation, if you succeed, it is only your success and when you fail, it is your failure only. You cannot make somebody else a scapegoat or blame others for your failure; and this situation is like cursing oneself. But a true leader takes responsibility for his success and failures both. This is the reason that when Warren Buffett's investments in two Ireland banks had failed and when he had bought shares of stock of multinational power corporation Conoco Phillips Company at high prices, it was his failure only. And Warren had even publicly owned the mistakes. This is the reason that Warren Buffett always picks managers/ chief executive officers who are ready to own both their success and failures.

A Manager Needs to Have Many More Traits

Warren Buffett looks for many traits while picking the right managers'.

Do they love their job? Buffett makes sure that the person whom he is entrusting his business is doing what he loves to do. There is a very interesting Buffett's quote, *"There comes a time when you ought to start doing what you want. Take a job that you love. You will jump out of bed in the morning. I think you are out of your mind if you keep taking jobs that you don't like because you think it will look good on your resume. Isn't that a little like saving up sex for your old age?"*

In fact, many times we keep doing things that we do not like, just looking for money. But the irony is that we keep doing the same job day-after-day, year-after-year, until we reach end of our time. In the meantime, we keep ourselves under the misconception that we would eventually attain our dream job. This pain, in the name of earning, starts right in the initial years of one's life and is fore casted based on needs. If we look at the psychology behind the same, it would be clear that nothing but greed is behind this kind of pain. Warren believes not doing what we love in the name of greed is poor management of our lives. This state of our mind makes our job a hard labour, pushes us down and destroys our soul. We may be earning a lot, but 9-10 hours that we spend doing that are quite painful.

In the world of business, the people who are most successful are those who are doing what they love. The interesting fact is that the thing that always motivates them is not money. It is that same thing that motivates a singer to sing and a player to play - love for one's job. Irrespective of what you are - a carpenter, barber, butcher, salesman, security man, computer programmer, doctor, chartered accountant, lawyer or anyone else - you can attain any level of success if you really love what you do. Such people only earn the most money and fame in their profession. Obviously, loving what you do and attaining success and money - they both go together.

That is why Warren Buffett makes sure while choosing managers/chief executive officers that they are assigned the job they love. Such people only feel happiness and pride in their jobs, motivate their colleagues to bring out their potentials and become driving force for the entire business. And their collective strength has only made Warren Buffett a great brilliant leader of this time.

Does he believe in his product? Warren Buffett, in the initial years of his professional life, had learnt that only salesmen who believe in their products are the best. People who are passionate about their products enjoy selling them and their sale levels are always high. Such people are equally interested in related matters like raw materials, production process, best utilisation etc. And salesmen who are familiar with all details relating to their products are able to easily impress their consumers. In his companies, Buffett has assembled such people only who believe in their products and businesses. This is the reason that majority of the chief executive officers in associate companies of Berkshire Hathaway have spent most of their professional life in managing a single company. The interesting fact is also that most of them have huge personal wealth.

In this context, the name of Buffalo News publisher Stanford Lipsey who was born and brought up in Omaha comes first; he worked with Warren Buffett for more than four decades. In 1969, Buffett had acquired 'Sun Newspapers', the group of local weekly newspapers founded and managed by Lipsey. In 1980, Buffett had appointed him as the publisher of Buffalo News where he continued at the same job for next 32 years and retired in 2012. He died four years later in 2016. Similarly, Irvin Blumkin had started working in 1967 at the age of eight in Nebraska

Furniture Mart founded by his grandmother Rose Blumkin (Mrs B); his father Louie Blumkin was looking after operations there. Irvin assumed charge as CEO during 1980s and he along with his brother Ron Blumkin has been managing the business since then. These people were so rich individually that they could have taken retirement any time. But Irvin, just like Lipsey, was also passionate about his work. Irvin's grandmother was active till the age of 103 and his father Louie Blumkin is still the chairman emeritus. It is worth reminding that Buffett had in 1983 acquired 80 per cent ownership stake from Blumkin family but he has continued to retain business control of Nebraska Furniture Mart with the family members as before and they all love what they do. They believe in their products.

Is he passionate about his work? In Warren's view, "He is a great manager who thinks of business when he gets out of bed in the morning and dreams about the business when he sleeps in the night". He believes, "Obsession is the price of perfection". Warren expects obsession not only from his managers but he himself has also been obsessive his entire life. It was his obsession only that Warren was able to memorise Moody's Manual and even today, he is always ready with all the figures related to all his businesses. Warren had bought Nebraska Furniture Mart as the same was being managed by an obsessive lady like Mrs B who had made even her children obsessive.

Now, if we have a look at the professional life of Olza M. Tony Nicely, Chairman & CEO of motor vehicle insurance company Government Employees Insurance Company (GEICO), we find that he started working there as a clerk in 1961, at the age of just 18. Going up the ladder, he reached the current position in 1993. Thus, Tony had spent 56 years working for the same company. He is now going to cross 74 and his personal net worth is estimated to be USD 15 million (January 2017). Still, he himself never knew when he would retire, as obsessive people like Tony keep working till their mind and body are functional. And Buffett likes such managers only.

Somewhat similar story is that of Albert Lee 'Al' Ueltschi, founder of the world's foremost aviation training organisation 'FlightSafety International'. After listening to the radio broadcast of Charles Lindbergh's solo transatlantic flight in 1927, Albert Ueltschi got obsessed with flying. Then, he opened a hamburger stand named 'Little Hawk'to pay for flying lessons. He had started making solo flights at the age of 16. Very soon, he dropped out of his classes at the University of Kentucky to move around the country to provide flight training to student pilots, and finally began his career as a pilot with Pan American World Airways (Pan Am). After flying for 10 years there, Ueltschi felt that corporate pilots did not receive the same rigorous training that airline pilots received and at the age of 50, he founded Flight Safety International in 1951. By the time the company went public 17 years later in 1968, Ueltschi was considered the 'father of modern flight training'. In 1996, Ueltschi sold majority stake in his company to Warren Buffett in exchange for 16000 shares of Berkshire Hathaway at USD 1.50 each; however, Buffett ensured that Ueltschi remained connected to the company for his entire life.

At the time Al Ueltschi died in 2012 at the age of 95, Flight Safety International was operating more than 4000 individual courses for 135 kinds of planes through 1800 trainers and was using more than 320 flight simulators to offer services to its customers in 167 countries. Warren Buffett had later commented about Ueltschi, "Al understood what I was doing. I knew the mission of Flight Safety and I could say he loved his profession. The first question that I ask about the position of an individual is - does he love money or his profession? But, for Al money was entirely insignificant. He loved his profession and he was the kind of person I need; had he loved money he would have left the company very next day it was sold".

Yes, the first thing that Warren Buffett always tries to find out about his prospective manager is whether he has been loving his profession ever since his childhood. Buffett believes that if a manager has taken more interest in some petty profession than his studies during his childhood, he may be able to achieve better success as compared to many educated managers, as his childhood love for a profession makes him passionate to succeed. Thus, the first thing Buffett looks for in his manager is how much he loves his job and how passionate he is about the same; and if he is educated and has other skills also, that comes as the icing on a cake.

How loyal and honest he is? Buffett believes if a worker or manager is loyal and honest towards others, there are greater chances of him correcting himself by learning from others. On the contrary, if a worker or manager overlooks his mistakes or tries to blame others for his mistakes, it is quite probable that he would lie to himself in other important matters also and there would be no possibility of him getting corrected. Buffett believes "Managers that always promise to 'make the numbers' will at some point be tempted to make up the numbers". This was the reason that he would shy away from picking managers who discussed more about their employment contracts than work. He maintained that it was not possible to do business with people who get excited by their contracts. In the business world, a manager honest as the brightness of the day is like balance lying in your bank account. And Buffett would always look for such managers only.

Can he do cost-management? Profit is the life blood of business. Just as end of blood circulation brings end to life, end of flow of profit stops the business, and the only way to maintain profit flow is to keep production cost lower than the sale price as much as possible. The difference between sale price and production cost is what is known as profit margin. There cannot be any other way or formula for making profit. If you are unable to maintain your profit margin, you are definitely not going to last in business for long. And if you are able to make great profits, you may not only earn your livelihood but also become affluent.

As the manager of a business, a person has mainly two goals - sell products at maximum prices by motivating sales team to improve sales and keep production costs at the lowest level by motivating teams procuring products and raw materials. It is most important to keep production costs to the lowest level as they only determine sale prices. It may be easy to sell a product with low production cost in good quantities and thus maintain better profit margin. In such a case, if a business manager is not 'watchful about costs', it would not be possible for him to maintain costs at the lowest level. Buffett maintains that a manager not disciplined for little things would be undisciplined in more significant matters also.

In this context, Warren Buffett narrates stories of Tom Murphy, CEO of Capital Cities Communications; he was so conscious of costs that he had not allowed painting of the rear wall of his office building, as the same was not visible to anybody. Not only that, Murphy never created public relations and legal departments in his office, as he believed these services could be obtained from freelance professionals whenever required at very low costs. And when Murphy merged Capital Cities into ABC, he had even closed personal dining rooms along with other cost cuttings.

Does he have a long-term perspective? Warren Buffett says, "In fact, managing and investing have lot of overlapping. Managing has made me a better investor and investing a better manager".

Yes, Warren Buffett has always been a long-term investor. He has always tried to maintain his majority stake in favourite companies providing durable competitive advantage, as their inherent economics work in their favour. Warren's this very long-term perspective has made him such a great and successful investor. However, most of the managers in corporate world work with short-term perspective, as their performances are measured by their quarterly and annual results. If they surpass their estimated quarterly or annual performance, they are rewarded with fat bonuses and promotions, and if they fail to reach those quarterly or annual targets, their jobs are in danger.

In Buffett's view, such short-term perspective of management kills long-term potentials of the business. He calls this management perspective as 'reactive management' and tries to keep himself away from the same. Buffett believes that management should be proactive, not reactive. He has attained great success as an investor by adopting long-term perspective only, and hence he has implemented this very perspective in his acquired businesses also. The most important point in his prefatory instructions that Buffett conveys to his managers after appointment is that they should stop worrying about short-term ups and downs of the business and concentrate on making the business strong and profitable in the long-term.

At the time Warren Buffett acquired Berkshire Hathaway, it was an average grade company that was making capital investments more than its income in a desperate bid to compete with foreign textile manufacturers. He soon realised that textile manufacturing required continuous capital investments though its chances of making profit was quite low. Hence, he stopped spending on working capital of Berkshire's textile production and used that capital to acquire an insurance company that had much better potentials in long-term perspective.

How? This was a result of Buffett's intensive study of inherent economics of various businesses. We have already seen this in the first chapter. Buffett was well aware that the textile industry required constant capital infusion to stay in business and that it was eating away income and preventing the company to become profitable. Hence, Buffett knew that any extent of capital investment in Berkshire would not have made any significant impact on its profitability. On the other side, constant cash flow is maintained in insurance business through premiums whereas the claim payments are comparatively quite less. Building an insurance network requires one-time capital investment that is negligible in comparison to manufacturing businesses. Thus, an insurance company always has a good amount of cash for investment in other profitable avenues. This was the reason that Buffett had eventually stopped all textile manufacturing activities of Berkshire and started to gradually transform it into a financial powerhouse. And this is the reason Buffett directs his managers to manage businesses with a long-term perspective.

Provision of Performance-Based Emoluments- Buffett says, "If you have a great manager, you want to pay him well". But how much? Buffett has a simple formula to decide compensation for his managers. He compares the performance of his manager against average performance of the related industry. Obviously, only if Buffett's manager delivers a performance better than industry average, he considers the manager worthy of bonus. If for some reasons, the company fails to achieve industry average, Buffett finds out how much the manager has contributed towards making the company strong and profitable with long-term perspective and determines manager's annual bonus based on the same. He considers his manager an expert coach in different sports. Just as inherent economics of different sports are not the same and coaches of all sports are not paid the same salary, Buffet determines compensation for his managers of various businesses based on financial potentials of related businesses.

❑

4

Motivation of Workforce

Warren Buffett had realised, right at the start of his professional life, that once he had chosen the right businesses and entrusted full authority for their operation to right managers, the only job he was left with as the owner and leader of the businesses was - to constantly motivate the managers for their outstanding performance. Yes, Buffett's management motivational skills have played a major role in transforming Berkshire Hathaway into a financial powerhouse. In this chapter, we are going to discuss in detail these very Buffett's skills - what all he learnt from the father of 'self-improvement' Dale Harbison Carnegie and others and how he adopted them in his winning management style. Be it the skill of impressing others in very first meeting or magic of using appreciation or risk of using criticism or precise use of counselling - Warren Buffett is placed at the top of the most skilled leaders of this age in terms of encouraging, motivating and influencing his managers.

Impact of Friendly Gesture in First Meeting

Warren Buffett says, "You should open talk in a friendly manner when you meet somebody the first time". Though Buffet has just repeated the age-old saying about practical skills "First impression is the last impression", he has used the same successfully to leave a magical influence on his managers.

Beryl B Raff, Chairperson and CEO of Helzberg Diamond Shops, a subsidiary of Berkshire Hathaway, has recounted her first meeting with Warren Buffet in an interesting way in her interview (1 May 2014) published in Kansas City Business Journal. It was sometime in 2009 when she was working as Executive Vice President in Fine Jewellery Division of American departmental store chain J C Penny. Starting her professional career in 1975, Beryl Raff was one of the most experienced workers in retail jewellery business. An acquaintance had asked Beryl Raff about her interest in the interview for the position of chief executive officer of Helzberg Diamond. It is worth noting that Helzberg Diamond, founded in 1915 by Morris Helzberg, operated 270 diamond jewellery retail stores across the United States of America and Warren Buffet had acquired the company in 1995.

Beryl Raff was fully aware of the distinguished history of Helzberg Diamond and she was also a long-time admirer of Warren Buffet; she was also aware of Buffett's well-known working style and excellent quality of the professionals working with him for long. She could not ignore this great opportunity to work for a world-famous leader like Buffett. For her, just having the opportunity to talk to Buffett for some time was itself not less than the greatest achievement of her life. And when she landed at Omaha airport for interview, she had never imagined that Warren Buffett himself would be waiting there in his golden Cadillac to receive her.

Naturally, Beryl was quite nonplussed, but Buffett soon allowed her to calm down with his simple behaviour. She found Buffett a jovial and attractive person and she quickly got rid of her fear. At Berkshire headquarters, Buffett asked her many questions relating to jewellery business. After spending few hours there, he took Beryl to his favourite Omaha Club for lunch. After that, he took her around his hometown and finally also offered her the position of Chairperson and CEO of Helzberg Diamond

Shops. All this was just like a dream for Beryl. She however composed herself and asked Buffett, "Would I be reporting to you?" He responded, "No, you wouldn't report directly to me. You do not report to anybody. It is your company. You run it, and if you ever want to talk about anything, just call me".

Warren Buffett had chosen Beryl Raff as his manager, but Buffett's simplicity had made Beryl so stunned that she just could not say anything at that moment. Buffett's words were still echoing in her ears when she took return flight for Dallas. She was finding herself unable to believe her luck. Beryl took 2-3 days to come to senses and she conveyed Buffett her acceptance of his offer. In his press note released on 6 April 2009 from Berkshire Hathaway headquarters, Warren Buffett announced appointment of Beryl Raff, "Beryl is widely recognised in the retail industry as an outstanding merchant and a strong multi-store retail executive. In her new position, she would bring with her finely balanced blend of merchandising instinct and analytical sharpness".

And within just a few months after taking charge at Helzberg Diamond, Beryl Raff realised that she had already been accepted as a member of Warren Buffet's extended family. Yes, this was the result of Buffett's management motivational skills that impressed her in the very first meeting. Just imagine what would have been the impression on Beryl if Buffett had not gone himself to receive her or he had not shown warmth in his behaviour or had not personally taken her around the city or for lunch. Beryl might have still worked for Helzberg Diamond as she was getting a great professional opportunity and was going to be a part of a mega financial empire like Berkshire, but she would not have considered Warren Buffett anything more than the billionaires interested only in their business profits. Buffett has been understanding this psychology quite well - if you want to have your own way, you must start off your interaction with people in friendly manner only. And this management motivational skill has played a major role in helping Buffett assemble a group of the world's best professionals.

Magic of Appreciation in Human Resource Management

Warren Buffet says, "We all have a deep and genuine craving to be appreciated". Yes, Buffett always understood well the practical psychology of the magic of appreciation in human resource management. He recognises this psychological fact that we all have a natural basic need to feel important. To a great extent, this is also a biological need of every human being. There is a famous quote of William James, referred to as the 'Father of American psychology' and counted among the greats of psychological and pragmatic philosophical traditions of 20th century, that says, "The deepest principle of human nature is the craving to be appreciated".

However, Warren Buffett had learnt about the amazing power of appreciation in human resource management after studying the management skills of the legendary professional of American steel industry Charles Michael Schwab. He had started his professional career as a simple labour in Edgar Thomson Steel Works and Furnaces (Braddock, Pennsylvania) of American steel magnate Andrew Carnegie. Impressed by his diligence, hard work and leadership skills, Carnegie was constantly assigning him major responsibilities. However, Schwab had given the best demonstration of his abilities when Carnegie assigned him the responsibility of setting things right at Homestead Steel Works, a large steel plant suffering from labour troubles. He brought about amazing reforms in its financial condition as well as labour-management relations. In 1897, at only 35 years of age, he became president of the Carnegie Steel Company. Soon, Carnegie Steel grew to be the world's largest steel company. In 1901, he played a significant role in negotiating the historical deal of USD 480 million (equivalent to USD 14.1 billion in 2016) for sale of Carnegie Steel to a group of New Yorkbased financiers led by J. P. Morgan, and later also became the president of the United States Steel Corporation, the company formed out of Andrew Carnegie's former holdings. However, after several clashes with J. P. Morgan and his supporter fellow executive Elbert Gary, Schwab left USS in 1903 and took charge of the Bethlehem Shipbuilding and Steel Company (Bethlehem, Pennsylvania). Under his leadership, Bethlehem Steel soon became USS's biggest competitor and second largest steel company of the United States of America.

Yes, Charles Michael Schwab was the first highly successful manager and chief executive officer who was paid an annual remuneration of USD 1 million. By 1920s, Schwab's fortunes had reached the level of USD 200 million. Though Schwab's luxurious lifestyle, shoddy investments and the Great Depression had robbed his fortunes and he was almost broke at the time of his death in 1936, professionals around the world even today acknowledge his management skills. The interesting fact is that Schwab was not recognised as the most respected manager of his time just because he was the greatest specialist of steel industry but also because he had an extraordinary ability to motivate his workers and he did the same using appreciation and encouragement. Schwab had once said, "I consider my ability to arouse enthusiasm among my people the greatest asset I possess, and the way to develop the best that is in a person is by appreciation and encouragement. There is nothing else that so kills the ambitions of a person as criticism from superiors. I never criticise anyone. I believe in giving a person incentive to work. So I am anxious to praise but loath to find fault. If I like anything, I am hearty in my appreciation and lavish in my praise".

Charles Michael Schwab had learnt all this from his boss Andrew Carnegie. Carnegie never hesitated in appreciating his workers not only privately but also publicly. Warren Buffett follows this advice from Schwab as if appreciating workers and managers for small things and being too enthusiastic with them on major affairs are religious tenets. Yes, Buffett has been hearty in his appreciation of his workers and has been their greatest admirer. He never misses a chance to appreciate his managers privately or in Berkshire's annual public meetings and annual reports. Yes, this is what Buffet has learnt from Schwab - if you appreciate people even for petty things, they would present to you much bigger achievements in coming times to get your appreciation. Thus, in Buffett's view, appreciation and praise are priceless gifts that always give something much bigger in return. Obviously, if you expect to constantly receive something great from your employees, you must keep on showering them with your praise and appreciation on regular basis.

Importance of Living with Your Dignity

Warren Buffet had learnt from the world's greatest steel magnate Andrew Carnegie the importance of allowing his workers to live with dignity. In this context, he often narrates the story told by Carnegie and impresses upon his managers to ensure that they themselves as well as the people working with them are able to live with dignity.

Carnegie's story goes like this. A manager was working with a trustworthy old employee. Monotony of job had made the employee slack in his work. This had resulted in fall in his workmanship and productivity. The manager reviewed his performance. He could have shown the employee the door, but in that case he would have had to work in his place. The manager could have even threatened the employee to fire him but being an old worker, this would have made him upset. In the situation, the manager talked to the experienced employee directly in a friendly manner. The manager, during the conversation, mentioned him as the best employee and the one who inspired other workers. The manager also told him that even many customers appreciated his workmanship. In the end, the manager calmly conveyed to him that he was rapidly falling behind in his work for the last few days. The manager let the employee know that he was worried for him and was wondering if he could help him in any manner. The manager thus provided the employee an opportunity to realise his old dignity again. Obviously, this was going to have a positive impact. Everybody likes to live with dignity. After that meeting, the employee started showing sudden improvement in his work behaviour. He got rid of the boredom. He started to work with his old enthusiasm. He soon attained his earlier productivity levels and people started to appreciate his workmanship once again.

Sitting at the top of a huge business empire, when Warren Buffet appreciates his CEOs publicly, he actually encourages them to live with dignity. Buffett knows very well that when a manager tries to live with dignity, he would inspire his employees also to do the same, like the story above.

Buffett had even suggested Ireland's rock band U2's lead vocalist and primary lyricist Paul David Hewson, known by his stage name 'Bono', that if he wanted to secure encouraging assistance and financial support from Americans to fight poverty in Africa, he should have appealed to their 'greatness' rather than awakening their 'conscience'. In fact, Bono is counted among the world's most distinguished philanthropist actors and is known as the most politically effective celebrity of all time. Since 1999, Bono has been active in raising awareness of the plight of Africa and AIDS. In this regard, he met several influential politicians, including former US President George W. Bush and former Canadian Prime Minister Paul Martin. In March 2002, after meeting with Bono, George W Bush had announced from the White House a financial assistance of USD 5 billion to Africa and had remarked, "This is a significant first step and a serious and effective level of commitment.... this should happen immediately as this is a crisis".In the same year, Bono had taken US Secretary of the Treasury Paul H. O'Neill on a tour to four African countries. In the same course, Bono had met Warren Buffett and had sought his advice on making Americans aware of his campaign. In an interview published in 'US Today' (15 September 2003), Bono had revealed Buffett's advice to him, "Do not appeal to the conscience of America, appeal to its greatness, you'll get the job done".

If you notice, you may find why Warren Buffett advised Bono to appeal to America's 'greatness' and not to its 'conscience'. In fact, when we try to awaken anybody's conscience, we indirectly try to awaken his or her sense of 'right' and 'wrong'. Thus, when Bono was appealing to the conscience of Americans, he was indirectly telling them, "What kind of humans are you if you are not ready to help the poor and hungry in Africa?" And hence, though unknowingly, Bono was playing with the sense of guilt of the Americans and rebuking them. Obviously, nobody would like a person who stirs up his sense of guilt and rebukes him. And that was the reason he was not getting expected response from the Americans in his campaign.

After that, Bono changed the tone of his appeal during his American music programmes, "You are the most intelligent nation on this earth. You won the World War II against all odds and created hole in the heaven to land man on the Moon. Faced with the serious issue of helping the Africans who were in poverty and pain and had lost their souls, I wondered whom I should turn to? I had then felt a manifestation of Lord Jesus. I should turn to the greatest nation of the world - the kind of people who can really solve tough problems, the nation that can attain the impossible". Obviously, Bono had appealed to the greatness of America and its distinguished reputation at the advice of Buffett. And, he really got his job done. After that, many individuals and social service organisations including 'Melinda Gates Foundation' had wholeheartedly donated for Bono's campaign.

Obviously, Warren employed the same psychology for expansion of his financial empire. He has tried to appeal to the greatness of his managers instead of awakening their sense of guilt, as he knows well that if you appeal to others' greatness, they would always work in your interest. Of course, Warren's managers and employees have done the same thing to him.

Grave Dangers of Criticising Your Own People

Warren Buffett says, "Use of criticism for motivation is useless, as it makes a person defensive, hurts his precious pride, impairs his sense of importance and arouses discontent". Buffett is aware of this psychological truth that uncalled-for criticism is something that we hate to hear. This generates discontent. This may force people even to leave their parents' house. This is the main reason behind failed marital relationships. Still, most of us keep showering others, especially the people at our workplaces, with uncalled-for criticism. Managers and leaders of work-groups often make this mistake of publicly criticising their own people with the aim of motivating them. However, Buffett had understood right at the beginning of his professional life that uncalled-for criticism could never motivate anybody. This could not bring about durable change in a person and this demolished all kinds of productive work-relationships.

This is the reason that when any of the managers at Berkshire makes a mistake, Warren Buffett first of all tries to understand what made the manager to make that mistake. He looks at his manager and his work situation and tries to visualise things by putting himself in his position. This helps him to make out the real purpose of that risky management decision. If the manager has taken a calculated risk with the aim of doing something good, Buffett has an amazing capacity to withstand even huge losses on account of such occasional mistakes committed by the managers.

In this context, the case of rise and fall of David L. Sokol, Chairman and CEO of Mid American Energy Company (Des Moines, Iowa), a subsidiary of Berkshire Hathaway, and regarded as the likely successor to Warren Buffett, is worth mentioning. Raised in Buffett's hometown Omaha and civil engineering graduate from Nebraska University (Omaha), Sokol started his professional life from an architectural engineering firm. In 1982, Sokol was appointed in Citi Bank (New York City) where he advised customers about investment in large waste-energy projects. After that he moved to energy-to-waste business with USD 500,000 seed money of a real estate company named Ogden. In the next six years, this had become a corporation earning revenue of USD 1 billion with more than 1000 employees and two plants at Oklahoma and Oregon, and had gone public in 1989. Thus Sokol, at just 32 years of age, became the CEO of a company listed in New York Stock Exchange. However, he was shown the door in 1990 after an altercation with the son of Ogden director. Sokol then joined JWP, a contractor company in New York, as president. He resigned from there in 1992 after an argument with the board of directors on accounting related issues.

This was the time when David L. Sokol was contacted by Walter Scott, CEO of Omaha based national construction company Peter Kiewit Sons. Walter had earlier worked for Ogden. Walter requested him to return to Omaha and work along with him on something new. Thus, Scott-Sokol partnership launched a small geothermal business that later took the shape of the large and profitable Mid American Energy company. Buffett's childhood friend Walter Scott, who was also a member in the Board of Directors of Berkshire, then made David Sokol also a part of Buffett's expanded family. In 2000, Berkshire acquired 80% ownership of Mid American. After that, Sokol executed many successful acquisitions and besides two-third ownership of Mid American Iowa, expanded his services to parts of Illinois, South Dakota and Nebraska. During the next 10 years, Buffett had compensated Sokol with a total of USD 8.8 million as salary and USD 53.9 million as bonus for his hard work. During the same period, Sokol had also received dividends of USD 26.3 million on his shares of stock and had sold shares amounting to USD 145.5 million.

In the meantime, in 2010, Douglas County (Nebraska) Judge Gary Randall found Mid American guilty of acting in 'improper, wrongful and unscrupulous manner' in its dealing with the shareholders of an irrigation project in Philippines and held David Sokol responsible for the same. Overall, Mid American had to pay 7% of its net profit of 2010 (around USD 84 million) as compensation. However, in his statement on 30 March 2011, Warren Buffett had also congratulated David Sokol and his confidant Gregory E. Obel for the excellent performance of Berkshire's public utility companies. It is worth reminding that David Sokol had made a grave investment error between 2002 and 2004 and Warren Buffet had on 13 September 2004 announced writing off a loss of USD 340 million in Mid American's Zinc Recovery Project. Buffett had not awarded any punishment in both the cases, as he did not find in them any intentional mistake by Sokol.

Not only that, earlier on 26 February 2011, Buffett in his annual letter to the shareholders of Berkshire, had credited David Sokol for financially rescuing Berkshire's subsidiary company Net Jets during the previous two years. Net Jets (Columbus, Ohio) operates the world's largest fleet of 700 private commercial jets and sells their part ownerships to its clients. In 1995, Warren Buffet had bought 25% share in 'Hawker 1000'. He had soon determined that the concept of part ownership was the future of private aviation and in 1998, Berkshire had acquired the entire company. But, when total pre-tax loss of Net Jets rose to the level of USD 157 million in the next eleven years, Buffett had appointed David Sokol as its CEO to turn it around. Buffett had indicated in his above letter that Net Jets loss would have been several hundred million greater, but for the backing of valuable goodwill of Berkshire. But, Sokol had turned the company around within a year. Sokol had carried out large scale retrenchment, sale of assets and fundamental changes in management to bring Net Jets to a position of pre-tax profit of USD 207 million in 2010.

In fact, Sokol had made a lot of money for Buffett and that had developed a lot of self-confidence in his ability. Besides managing Berkshire companies, Sokol had also explored opportunities for their investments. After the deepening crisis of Wall Street in 2008, Sokol had spent most of his time as a representative of Buffett for evaluation of potential deals created out of economic chaos. As per the 2010 report of US Bankruptcy Court on Lehman, Lehman Brothers' Chief of Investment Banking Hugh E. McGee III had contacted David Sokol in September 2008 to enquire if he had any idea or advice for saving Lehman. On getting a 'No' from Sokol. Lehman had filed for bankruptcy.

However, after the fall of Lehman, Sokol had brought to Buffett's attention the rapidly falling prices of shares of

Baltimore's utility company Constellation Energy Group(CEG) and after receiving Buffett's consent, Sokol as the chief of Mid American had almost pulled off the deal at heavily discounted price of USD 4.7 billion to acquire CEG and save the same from bankruptcy. However, before the process of acquisition could start, a French competitor had entered the fray with higher bid. But Sokol's hard work and foresight did not go waste. CEG had to compensate Berkshire with a payment of over USD 1 billion towards breakup fee and other terms of the deal. Thus, Sokol was successful in making a good amount of money for Buffet within a short span of few months.

Yes, this kind of 'profitable opportunism' has been a major part of the investment formula of Berkshire (Warren Buffett); this however gets very little appreciation. Buffett is reputed to be a 'generous owner' that lays emphasis on efficient management and puts the same in practice. As a result, many of the companies remain eager to get acquired by Berkshire. Not only this, Buffett's personal aura and the record of his previous achievements open for him the doors for such non-ownership investments that others can only dream of. Among the typical examples of such non-ownership investments are the deals in 2008 for Goldman Sachs (USD 5 billion) and General Electric (USD 3 billion) when both the companies had gone financially broke. Buffett had shown his goodwill towards the two companies at such a highly sensitive moment; but in return, Berkshire could earn, besides repayment of its principal (USD 8 billion), more than USD 4 billion towards redemption fee and warranty fee along with interest. Can other regular investors secure such profitable deals? And, David Sokol had played a significant role in all these deals.

But Warren Buffett surprised everybody on 30 March 2011 when he announced that David Sokol was going to tender his resignation from Berkshire. Later, 27 April, Berkshire's audit committee had released 18-page report wherein it had charged Sokol of violation of company standards by misleading Berkshire about his personal shares in chemicals manufacturer Lubrizol (LZ) that he had recommended to Buffett as an acquisition target. The committee had concluded that Sokol had committed the crime of 'Insider Trading' under Federal Law when he bought Lubrizol shares for USD 1 million in January and then recommended acquisition of the same company to Buffett. Of course, it would not have been easy for Warren Buffett to take the decision of Sokol's removal. Sokol had made mistakes earlier also and Buffett had been condoning them, as nothing came out of his investigations that could prove that the mistakes were made intentionally. But this was the first instance where Sokol had made the mistake for his personal gain; this had dented Berkshire's historical reputation and Buffett had to take the decision to remove him.

Praise by Name, Criticise By Category

Buffett knows very well that 'praise' and 'criticism' are two most important tools for any manager. If he is able to use them properly, he can motivate his workers to work hard, be creative and attain great achievements. If the tools are used incorrectly, they may demolish enthusiasm, aspiration and creativity of employees at work and even ensure their failure. Buffett believes learning how to effectively use 'praise' and 'criticism' is the primary task of a manager. The manager who understands properly the sensitivity of these tools and the challenges of their use can get anything done by his colleagues and employees. Warren has been expert in utilising these tools. He has this simple rule - 'Praise by name, criticise by category".

We all like to be appreciated. We crave appreciation as a child from parents, as a student from teachers and later as employee from seniors. We need appreciation from all of them, as we want to know if we are on the right path and this also inspires us to move ahead and do still better. On the contrary, nobody wants to hear his criticism. Whether we do anything or not, there is nothing more frightening that our own criticism. This is generally enough to destroy our enthusiasm. We were not ready as children to listen to our own criticism and now even as adults, we are not able to tolerate the same, as criticism proves us wrong. Be it parent or teacher or senior, we are unable to have regard for the person that criticises us and then, we start ignoring their words. Obviously, there is nothing greater than 'praise' to win friends and nothing greater than 'criticism' to make enemies. Now it all depends on you whether you want to appreciate somebody and make friends with him or criticise him to turn him into your enemy.

Many of the managers are never able to learn how to use 'praise' and 'criticism' in their conversation. As a result, they quickly become unpopular among their colleagues and employees and managements soon show them the door. However, Warren Buffett is considered to be an expert in using 'praise' and 'criticism' quite precisely and he has been successful in motivating his managers through the same to give their best performances. As we have read earlier, Buffett never misses any small or big opportunity to appreciate his people. He is adept at memorising the names of his people and always praises them by their names. Pick any of the annual reports of Berkshire Hathaway and look at Buffett's detailed letter addressed to the shareholders, you will surely find, along with the review of performance of various businesses, mention of the names and works of the employees showing outstanding performance in those categories. Yes, Buffett boosts self-esteem of his people by publicly appreciating their achievements and inspires them to lead their life with their elevated goodwill. The language that Buffett uses to praise also indicates that he himself also enjoys doing that. However, he not only praises his managers but also offers them promotion and huge monetary benefits much more than their expectations. This way, he makes his people feel 'special' and encourages them to do still better. This is the reason that the managers at Berkshire always keep vying for their best performances, as if they are working not for money but for their 'self-esteem'.

Though Warren Buffett considers every personal criticism poisonous, he is a realist also. He agrees that criticism is essential in certain situations and the same cannot be cast aside. However, when a personal criticism is necessary, he follows

Dale Carnegie who advises that a person should be praised before he is criticised; according to him, people are not able to bear their criticism without a word of appreciation, and hence they just would not accept the same. But, when the good works of a person are appreciated profusely during conversation and then his mistakes are raised before him, he listens to the same, accepts them and also tries not to repeat them. Thus, if you are looking for a positive result of criticising a person, you should always start conversation with his appreciation.

Better to Avoid Conflicts and Arguments

Warren Buffett had learnt from Dale Carnegie that instead of arguing, it was better to agree with someone in order to win his confidence and have him listen to your ideas. Warren adopted this philosophy from the very beginning and he has been famous for trying to avoid conflicts and arguments. He has been well aware that you do not have to be at a higher position to win an argument. When you, in your attempt to win an argument with someone, pick his mistakes to correct him, he may even feel insulted and in that situation, instead of agreeing to your ideas, he may even get displeased with you.

In fact, when Buffett agrees to others' views in order to avoid conflict or argument, his primary aim is to respect their opinions even if the same are contradictory to his own views. And when Buffett, instead of arguing, accepts others' contradictory opinions, they feel comfortable and naturally get anxious to listen to his ideas. And this is the adroitness of Buffett; he is well aware that putting across your ideas to others is the first step towards winning an argument. As a securities salesman at the start of his career, he used to readily agree to the points raised by his potential customers.

In fact, invaluable ideas of Benjamin Franklin, one of the founding fathers of the United States of America, had played a significant role in shaping the academic growth and personal and professional lives of Buffett and his friend and Berkshire's

Vice Chairman Charlie Munger. Pick any of Berkshire's annual reports; you will certainly find some of Benjamin Franklin's quotes there. Franklin also was adept at avoiding arguments and respecting others' opinions. Possibly, that was what had influenced Buffett to adopt this strategy.

Talk About Others' Wants and Needs

Warren Buffett says, "When you want people to do something, think not what you want but think what they want". Yes, as a leader and business owner, the key to Buffett's management success lies in the fact that he has always been able to understand and discuss the needs and wants of his managers/chief executive officers. In this respect, Buffett was influenced by the great industrialist of 20th century and founder of Ford Motor Company Henry Ford. Ford has written in his autobiography, "If there is any one secret of success, it lies in the ability to get other person's point of view and see things from that person's angle as well as from your own".

Buffett had embraced this idea in his personal as well as professional life. When he wanted to discipline his children, he would talk about their needs instead of making comments on them. Like, when he wanted his children to mind their health and control their weight, he would propose a reward programme for the same. Buffett understood adolescent psychology quite well and he knew that the children would not listen to him until their cash requirements were met. Similarly, when Buffett tried to acquire a family-owned private company, he would first of all talk about the prestige of the owner in that business. In fact, Buffett understood this very well that besides selling his company at the maximum possible price, the owner also wanted to ensure that the company was going in the hands that was capable of carrying forward its reputation. This was the reason that even after acquiring companies, Buffett used to hand over the same to the same previous owners who took pride in managing them for life.

We have already seen this in the case of Nebraska Furniture; after acquiring 80% stake in the company, Buffett did not go for any change in its management team consisting of Mrs B and his sons and members of the same family are still managing the same. Similarly, after acquiring FlightSafety, Buffett offered its founder and chairman AL Ueltschi the opportunity to run the company for life. And Buffett more or less tried to do the same with other companies, as he wanted to maintain the owners' reputation for their businesses. Thus, Buffett fulfilled the needs and wants of those owners and in return for his investment and magnanimity, they produced amazing financial results.

Besides this, Warren Buffet also gives his managers the chance to set their own goals and standards. He does appoint people on jobs but does not tell them what they are expected to do. This way, he prompts his managers to come up with their own views. And when managers feel free to set their own goals and standards, they always try to set higher goals and standards to project a better image in the eyes of their boss. As such, managers do know that though Buffett does not tell them anything, his silence conveys a lot. While he permits his managers to have complete freedom and authority to work, his expectations from them are also equally high. He expects extraordinary performance from his managers. Buffett believes that when we ask somebody to do something, it indirectly amounts to an order only. And it is psychological truth that nobody likes to be ordered and an order restricts the potentiality of performance. This is the reason that, instead of passing orders to his managers, Buffett confronts them with a number of questions and managers pick up Buffett's expectations from these questions only. In fact, Buffett's questions are indirect 'orders' as he shies away from passing 'orders' directly.

And...Warren Buffett believes that everybody makes mistakes and hence, one should inculcate the habit of promptly accepting his mistakes so as to ensure its timely correction.

❑

5

Risks, Challenges and Opportunities

Warren Buffett maintains that roads of business are full of pitfalls and planning is required to avoid them; this is called 'plan of disaster'. Risks of too much debt, breach by employees, good thoughts going astray, unintentional mistakes, managing yes-men and missing opportunities - are all examples of those pitfalls and special management techniques are required to handle those risks and challenges. In Buffett's view, only when we manage all of them properly, we are able to see related business opportunities. Buffett had learnt all this the hard way. In this chapter, we are going to discuss Buffett's these very invaluable experiences that would help every leader to keep away from managerial risks and extricate himself from such situations.

Too Much Debt is Like a Gamble Only

In Buffett's view, the managers resorting to too much credit are actually gambling. The irony is that these managers mostly have the misconception that they would not encounter any financial pitfalls on the long roads of their businesses. But they do need special business plans to move ahead avoiding those financial pitfalls. However, Buffett, based on his experience, cautions that if a business, though being managed exceptionally well, over-utilises its leverage to avail loans expecting profits exceeding outstanding payables, it cannot always cheat or avoid its financial problems.

Buffett maintains that over-utilisation of 'leverage' results in banking disaster in the world economy every twenty years. Banks are the masters of 'leverage'. Whatever credits they extend are all out of funds received from depositors on credit. However, while they go for short-term borrowing from depositors, they have to extend long-term credits. This goes on smoothly till the time banks are able to keep adding new depositors. But when most of the depositors demand payment of their short term credits at the same time and banks are not in a position to honour their demand, a situation of banking crisis comes up. In economic scenario, such situations of change also create many opportunities. But we may be able to take advantage of such situations only if we have enough cash in hand. And economic swings may even prove to be disastrous if we have already availed too much of loans. Buffett believes such economic changes have been taking place always and will be coming up in future also. The question is - are we capable of withstanding those changes?

Warren Buffett says that leverage is quite tempting and always takes us to crisis. The question is - why is leverage so tempting? Because it can dramatically boost the performance of managers of a business provided, of course, the managers know how to use leverage. Suppose you are running a business that normally generates a profit of Rs 1 crore without depending on any credit. In the situation, you expect that an additional Rs 10 crore of investment may lift profit by Rs 2 crore. This is a very tempting situation. But the problem is that your business is not in a position to fund that transaction. But you may use the leverage of your business to easily secure Rs 10 crore on credit from investment bankers sitting in capital markets, as they keep waiting for such opportunities only. They would happily offer you loan provided you agree to pay them annual interest of

Rs 1 crore. This means that after paying Rs 1 crore out of gross profit of Rs 2 crore in your new venture, you would be earning a net profit of Rs 1 crore. Thus, you may be able to report a net profit of Rs 2 crore (Rs 1 crore from existing operations and additional Rs 1 crore from new business) in the balance sheet of your company. Your business would thus show a 100 per cent jump in performance over previous year and you would be in a position to claim sizeable bonus from your management.

However, you as manager would be able to continue with this game of boosting your performance by using the leverage of your business only up to the point conditions continue to be normal and you are able to generate profit as expected. But the moment economic conditions change and recession sets in, your game would start getting into a bad shape. You would not be able to generate your expected profit. It may be possible that you are not in a position to pay even the interest amount. In the situation, your performance bubble would burst and your business would get into a financial crisis, leading the company into a possible bankruptcy. How would your board of directors deal with you in such a situation? The plain answer to the same is that it would replace existing management and you would lose your job.

That is why Warren Buffett terms too much of credit a gamble and does not invest in companies that have heavy long-term debts. Yes, Buffett had never allowed Berkshire to get entangled into debts. He never uses borrowed funds to buy a business. He allows cash to get accumulated until he finds a definitely attractive deal. In this respect, Warren Buffett is a conservative businessman who never tries to increase his income by using borrowed capital.

Great Ideas Also May Prove to be Bad

In his professional life, Warren Buffett had found this saying of his guru Benjamin Graham - 'Good ideas may deliver worse results than bad ideas' - to be true. Graham believed that managers never knowingly worked on bad ideas, as bad ideas got killed in the very beginning. But good ideas are put into practice. If a good idea succeeds, it becomes tradition. And when an idea turns into tradition, nobody even thinks of the same resulting into a failure. In such a situation, good ideas start getting misused. And as no caution is exercised in this regard, misuse of good ideas keeps on growing until the entire system collapses.

For example, subprime mortgage loan was basically a good idea that allowed worthy individuals with marginal credit to buy houses. As these schemes selling mortgage loans provided opportunity to earn sizeable commissions, they started selling 'subprime mortgage loans' even to undeserving individuals by claiming them to be worthy. As such, the number of undeserving borrowers started going up. They were buying more than one house and brokers were getting the chance to earn more. This had started creating an environment of boom in the real estate market. Racing to meet their ambitious targets, banks had started to blindly accept proposals from brokers. Thus, the annual rate of growth of subprime mortgage loans went up from 8 per cent in 2004 to 20 per cent in 2006.

Just to remind, constantly increasing extravagant habits had lifted the ratio of debt to disposable personal income of average American family, that was hovering at 77 per cent in 1990s, to exceptionally high level of 127 per cent by the end of 2007, especially due to subprime mortgage loans. In the situation, when real estate prices, after peaking around middle of 2006, started falling down rapidly, borrowers were finding it difficult to re-finance their houses. Hence, they had to go for refinancing at higher interest rates resulting in their EMI sizes going up and payment defaults becoming common. As real estate prices were going down rapidly, financial institutions stopped investing in securities backed by subprime mortgage loans, thus creating a situation of loan crisis in the American banking system.

On 15 September 2008, the Lehman Brothers declared themselves bankrupt. After Goldman Sachs, Morgan Stanley and Merrill Lynch, this was the fourth largest investment bank in the United States, with 25000 employees worldwide. Lehman

Brothers had at that time USD 619 billion in assets and USD 619 billion in liabilities. Thus, Lehman Brothers became the largest victim of the financial crisis of 2008 and the biggest bankruptcy in history. As a result, within just one month in October 2008, stock markets around the world went through a historical loss of USD 10,000 billion in their market capitalisation.

In fact, Lehman Brothers traces its roots to a small grocery store opened by the German immigrant Henry Lehman in Montgomery (Alabama) in 1844. In 1850, Henry Lehman and his brothers Emanuel and Mayor founded Lehman Brothers. Though, in the following decades, unabated economic development of the United States of America provided ample opportunity to Lehman Brothers to prosper, it had to face many challenges also during that period. Lehman Brothers survived the railroad bankruptcies in the beginning of 19th century, the Great Depression of 1930s, two world wars, a capital shortage when it was spun off by American Express in 1994 and the long-term capital management collapse and Russian debt default of 1998. However, its headlong rush into subprime mortgage market proved to be a disastrous step that brought it to its knees.

In 2003 and 2004, when the US housing bubble was well under way, Lehman acquired five mortgage lenders including BNC Mortgage and Aurora Loan Services, which specialised in the most-risky Alt-A category loans extended to borrowers without full documentation. These acquisitions and jump in real estate business enabled Lehman revenues in capital markets to surge to 56% from 2004 to 2006; this was much more compared to the growth of other investment bankers. Lehman securitised USD 146 billion of mortgages in 2006 - a 10% increase from 2005. Though Lehman reported net profits every year 2005 onwards, it announced in 2007 a record net income of USD 4.2 billion on a revenue of USD 19.3 billion. In February 2007, Lehman stock price reached a record USD 86.18 per share, taking its market capitalisation to the level of USD 60 billion. In the meantime, loan defaults had reached a seven-year high and the crisis of subprime mortgage had become apparent. On March

14, 2007, when stock markets had their biggest one-day drop in five years, Lehman had reported record results for its first fiscal quarter.

However, Lehman's stock fell sharply as the credit crisis erupted in August 2007 with the failure of two Bear Stearns (New York based investment bank, securities trading and brokerage firm) hedge funds; during the same month, the company eliminated 2500 mortgage-related jobs and shut down its BNC unit. It also closed offices of Aurora Loan Services in three states. Even as the correction in the U. S. housing market gained momentum, Lehman continued to be a major player in the mortgage market. In 2007, Lehman underwrote more mortgage-backed securities than any other firm, accumulating a USD 85 billion portfolio that was four times its shareholders' equity. Though, in the fourth quarter, Lehman's stock rebounded as global equity markets reached new highs, but the company did not go for trimming its massive mortgage portfolio and thus, it had lost even the last chance to save itself. By the end of 2007, Lehman's degree of leverage - ratio of total assets and shareholders' equity - was 31 and with the deteriorating market conditions, its large mortgage securities portfolio was rapidly weakening its financial condition.

Later in March 2008, when Bear Stearns' - second largest investment banking firm underwriting mortgage-backed securities - was close to collapse, it was being widely anticipated that the king of mortgage loans Lehman Brothers was the next to fail and its shares plummeted nearly 48%. Confidence in the firm returned somewhat after an issue in April of preferred shares of stock - which were convertible into Lehman shares at a 32% premium to its concurrent price - yielded USD 4 billion. However, the company's stock resumed its decline as hedge fund managers started to question the valuation of Lehman's mortgage portfolio.

On June 9, 2008, Lehman reported a historical second-quarter loss of USD 2.8 billion. This was its first loss since it was spun off by American Express in 1994. The company also reported that it had raised USD 6 billion from investors. The company also informed that it had boosted its liquidity pool to USD 45 billion, decreased gross assets to USD 147 billion, reduced its exposure to residential and commercial mortgages by 20% and cut down leverage from a factor of 32 to 25. But the markets found all these measures to be just too little, too late. During the next few months, Lehman's management made unsuccessful overtures to a number of potential partners. The stock plunged 77% in the first week of September 2008.

On 10 September, the company reported USD 3.9 billion loss for the third quarter, including a USD 5.6 billion devaluation of its assets. On the same day, Moody's Investor Services announced that it was reviewing Lehman's credit ratings and opined that the only way for Lehman to avoid a rating downgrade would be to sell its majority stake to a strategic partner. All these developments led to a 42% plunge in Lehman's market price on September 11. Over the weekend, when Lehman was left with just USD 1 billion of cash, it even made a last-ditch effort with Barclays and Bank of America for a deal; and Lehman Brothers was left with no option other than declaring its bankruptcy on 15 September.

There is Ample Money Within the Scope of Law

Warren Buffet keeps on clearly telling his managers that a lot of money can be made while remaining within the scope of law. Of course, it requires being aggressive to make money, but you can do so while remaining within the limits of law. Experience has taught Buffett that when a manager breaks law in a bid to make too much money too soon, his single step exposes entire business to risk. In this context, it is worth mentioning the example of the US Treasury Bond scandal of 1991 when the very existence of the Wall Street's famous investment banking firm Salomon Brothers was in danger as two of its bond traders were found to have broken law. In the situation, Warren Buffett as the largest investor and director of the firm, had to step in and he somehow managed to save the company after paying a heavy fine of USD 290 million.

In fact, American investor Ronald Owen Perelman, notorious as 'takeover specialist', had started his bid in August 1987 to takeover Salomon Brothers by acquiring 12% stake of Minerals & Resources Corporation Limited (a subsidiary of mega South African group Anglo American) in the company. Ronald Owen Perelman, founder of MacAndrews & Forbes Incorporated, was listed among the world's richest persons in 2016 at 80th position with total personal assets of USD 12.2 billion. The Salomon Brothers' Chairman and CEO John Gutfreund had then contacted Warren Buffett. On 27 September 1987, Buffett had acquired 12% stake in Salomon Brothers for USD 700 million through Berkshire Hathaway. This was Buffett's largest investment in a single company till date. However, Salomon Brothers had to pay USD 809 million to buy back 12% shares to save itself from Perelman's takeover plot, i.e., Buffett had made this shareholding investment to help Salomon Brothers at a heavy discount of USD 109 million and that also in the form of Convertible Preferred Shares that could be converted to common shares of stock any time. And, Buffett had made this investment because John Gutfreund had helped him in many deals during the last few years. For the first time, Warren Buffett had joined the so-called 'greedy community' of the Wall Street that he had always been avoiding.

In less than a month after this deal, on 19 October 1987 (Black Monday), Hong Kong and European stock markets experienced sharp declines followed by crash of stock markets in the United States; the Dow Jones Industrial Average (DJIA) fell 508 points (22.6%). Market price of a share of Berkshire Hathaway, that was USD 4230 a week back, came down to USD 3170 on Monday; and the company lost USD 5 billion in its market capitalisation within a day. Warren Buffett's personal net worth went down by USD 342 million. However, it is interesting to note that Warren Buffett had sensed the unexpected bounce in the market and sold most of the shares in his portfolio at highest prices to accumulate a lot of cash that could be used for investments at extremely low prices.

Warren Buffet's rescue proved to be momentary for Salomon Brothers and it was going to face a lot of financial issues in coming days. But the biggest crisis came in 1991 when U. S. Treasury Deputy Assistant Secretary Mike Basham learned that Salomon trader Paul Mozer had been submitting false bids in an attempt to purchase more treasury bonds than permitted by one buyer during the period between December 1990 and May 1991. The case forced the Chairman and CEO John Gutfreund to lose his job in August 1991. Later, U. S. Securities and Exchange Commission (SEC) imposed a fine of USD 100,000 on John Gutfreund and barred him from serving as a chief executive of an investment banking or brokerage firm. Meanwhile, in the absence of John Gutfreund, Warren Buffett being the largest investor took charge of Salomon Brothers and provided all assistance in SEC investigation. Though SEC did not ban Salomon Brothers from buying Treasury securities, considering Buffett's previous reputation and his honest assistance in the entire episode, but levied a fine of USD 290 million to cover damages; this was a historical penalty at that time. After running Salomon for nine months, Buffett handed over charge to competent managers in the company. Eventually, Travelers Group acquired Salomon in 1997 for USD 9 billion and Warren Buffett sitting in Omaha headquarters felt a sigh of relief, as his investment of USD 700 million had more than doubled to USD 1.70 billion. However, for Warren Buffett, this was a bitter experience involving investment in a Wall Street firm and by 2001, he was fully out of Salomon. Travelers merged with Citi Group in 2007.

This experience, however, came in handy for Warren Buffett to caution his managers. He has been using this example to explain to his managers that breaking law for immediate profits can prove to be highly detrimental to personal professional life as well as to very existence of the business.

Successes More Important than Mistakes

Warren Buffett also did not drop out of heaven! He has also built his fortune by learning from mistakes. He says, "I make plenty of mistakes and I'll make plenty more mistakes, too. That's part of the game. You've just got to make sure that the right things overcome the wrong ones". You may not always escape mistakes, but yes, you may surely attain greater success by learning from them. Hence, wisdom lies in ensuring that your successes overcome your mistakes. But, if the equation turns opposite, you are sure to get caught in troubles. We may learn from Buffett's experience to take following precautions:

Do not take decisions in hurry: In his letter to the shareholders of Berkshire Hathaway in its 2011 annual report, Warren Buffett had referred to his mistake in making heavy investment in bonds of Energy Future Holdings. He had written, "A few years back, I spent about $2 billion buying several bond issues of Energy Future Holdings, an electric utility operation serving portions of Texas. That was a mistake – a big mistake. In large measure, the company's prospects were tied to the price of natural gas, which tanked shortly after our purchase and remains depressed. Though we have annually received interest payments of about $102 million since our purchase, the company's ability to pay will soon be exhausted unless gas prices rise substantially. We wrote down our investment by $1 billion in 2010 and by an additional $390 million last year. At yearend, we carried the bonds at their market value of $878 million. If gas prices remain at present levels, we will likely face a further loss, perhaps in an amount that will virtually wipe out our current carrying value. Conversely, a substantial increase in gas prices might allow us to recoup some, or even all, of our write-down. However things turn out, I totally miscalculated the gain/loss probabilities when I purchased the bonds. In tennis parlance, this was a major unforced error by your chairman".

Two years later, in the annual report for 2013, Warren Buffett had written to the shareholders of Berkshire Hathaway, "Most of you have never heard of Energy Future Holdings. Consider yourselves lucky; I certainly wish I hadn't. The company was formed in 2007 to affect a giant leveraged buyout of electric utility assets in Texas. The equity owners put up $8 billion and borrowed a massive amount in addition. About $2 billion of the debt was purchased by Berkshire, pursuant to a decision I made without consulting with Charlie. That was a big mistake. Unless natural gas prices soar, Energy Future Holdings (EFH) will almost certainly file for bankruptcy in 2014. Last year, we sold our holdings for $259 million. While owning the bonds, we received $837 million in cash interest. Overall, therefore, we suffered a pre-tax loss of $873 million. Next time I'll call Charlie".

Yes, Buffett's presumption was correct and EFH, acquired by private equity firms KKR, TPG Capital and Goldman Sachs Capital Partners in 2007, could not withstand the burden of debt amounting to more than USD 40 billion. This deal executed in anticipation of rise in gas prices proved to be too costly when, on 29 April 2014, EFH filed for bankruptcy. But, more than losing money, Buffett was regretting his mistake of not consulting his old friend and vice chairman of Berkshire before making his decision. There are very few people as fortunate as Buffett to have a friend like Charlie Munger for sharing ideas. However, we may certainly strive to avoid doing what Buffett did - he took a decision in a hurry. It is always better to take some time before finalising an investment decision, even if the same involves much less than Buffett's mistake of USD 2 billion. It may be noted that the mistake of USD 2 billion was quite insignificant compared to Buffett's achievements, and he could comfortably bear the same.

Make thorough analysis of company and industry: In 2015, Buffett had written to the shareholders of Berkshire about performance of manufacturing, services and retail operation of the company till date. Most of them, not all, had given good results. In most of the cases where companies were not doing well, he had accepted his mistake in evaluation of the company and related industry. Possibly, the most notable example of Buffett's error in evaluation of an industry was the main company Berkshire Hathaway. Berkshire was then a textile manufacturer and Buffett had a great opportunity to sell his shares and make good money. Instead, Buffett had continued with his investment in that textile company that he later accepted to be a dying business. Yes, Buffett had acquired Berkshire in 1965; but when textile operations were completely shut down in 1985, it was already 20 years since then. Thus, even an intelligent investor like Buffett may end up wasting time as well as money. This only proves that nobody can be always right. But this also does not mean that we keep ignoring facts and avoid taking hard steps. Hence, a thorough analysis of the company and related industry is imperative before making investments.

Check out competitions also thoroughly: In his 2015 annual letter to the shareholders of Berkshire, Buffett had mentioned that not checking out competitions before buying Dexter Shoes was one of his 'most gruesome mistakes' till date. Everything looked good when he bought the company in 1993. Buffett could not see foreign competition coming and the value of his initial investment of USD 44.3 billion in Dexter Shoes going to zero. The incident teaches us that, irrespective of the company you are buying the shares of or the industry that the same belongs to or the size of the investment, the first thing you need to check out is the competition existing in the related market segment. Keep in mind that every market segment is thronged by companies that were once strong but could not compete with the rivals having better quality, better speed and better prices.

Do not use well-invested fund to make fresh investments - More than his mistake of not checking out competitions before finalising deal for Dexter Shoe, Buffett regretted using shares of Berkshire Hathaway for the transaction. By the time Buffett informed the shareholders in 2014, the shares that he used to buy Dexter were worth USD 5.70 billion that was later going to rise further by 40%. This incident teaches an important lesson that a well-invested fund should not be used for investment elsewhere.

Here, the words of great ancient Indian economist Acharya Chankya look to be so apt, "योध्रुवाणिपरित्यज्यअध्रुवंपरिषेवते। ध्रुवाणितस्यनश्यन्तिअध्रुमनष्टमेवच।", i.e., whosoever leaves behind a task that can certainly be completed, and runs after another task completion of which is uncertain, not only the previous task gets spoiled but even the uncertain task would get spoiled. Yes, even prudent investors sometimes make grave mistakes of selling stocks earning them assured profits and investing the money in options with uncertain prospects. Hence, if a share of stock is giving good income and the related business has strong fundamentals, it is better to continue with the same.

Do not doubt yourself much: Berkshire Hathaway had acquired General Reinsurance Corporation (Gen Re) in 1998. Immediately after that, Warren Buffet started having doubts on his own decision. There were issues that prompted external observers feel that billionaire investor Buffett had made a grave mistake this time; but Buffett had not made any mistake in buying 'Gen Re'. Of course, the biggest mistake he was making was to 'doubt' his own decision because of the questions being raised by external observers. However, Buffett did not allow that 'doubt' to overwhelm his decision, as a re-evaluation had given him confidence that his decision was perfect as per basic investment principles and he did not have to heed external opinions. Fortunately, Buffett maintained confidence in his decision and in his own words, 'Gen Re' proved to be a 'gem' later. The incident provides the lesson that it is not proper for anybody to doubt himself too much. If you have bought any share based on sound investment principles, you may definitely review your decision based on external observations but should not doubt your decision over and over again. Keep in mind, you have taken the decision as per your perspective that needn't match those of others.

Avoid greed when it is time to sell: It is common perception that once Warren Buffett buys a stock, he holds the same 'forever'. But this is not entirely true. Leaving some exceptions, he keeps churning rest of the investment portfolio. In 2013, British multinational groceries and general merchandise retailer Tesco was included in the list of companies with maximum holdings in Berkshire's portfolio; but it completely disappeared from the list next year. Though Buffett had come to know of the management problems in Tesco in 2013 itself and he had even made profits by selling a part of his holding in the company, he had taken a lot of time, in the hope of things turning around, to sell rest of his holding. Thus, when it was time to sell, Buffett was gripped by greed of better returns in future. And as a result, Berkshire had to provide for a net loss of USD 444 million at the end of 2014 towards that deal.

In his letter to the shareholders in Berkshire Hathaway's annual report of 2014, Buffett had described the sequence of events like this, "Attentive readers will notice that Tesco, which last year appeared in the list of our largest common stock investments, is now absent. An attentive investor, I'm embarrassed to report, would have sold Tesco shares earlier. I made a big mistake with this investment by dawdling. At the end of 2012 we owned 415 million shares of Tesco, then and now the leading food retailer in the U.K. and an important grocer in other countries as well. Our cost for this investment was USD 2.3 billion, and the market value was a similar amount."

"In 2013, I soured somewhat on the company's then-management and sold 114 million shares, realising a profit of USD 43 million. My leisurely pace in making sales would prove expensive. Charlie calls this sort of behaviour 'thumb-sucking.' (Considering what my delay cost us, he is being kind.)"

"During 2014, Tesco's problems worsened by the month. The company's market share fell, its margins contracted and accounting problems surfaced. In the world of business, bad news often surfaces serially: You see a cockroach in your kitchen; as the days go by, you meet his relatives. We sold Tesco shares throughout the year and are now out of the position. (The company, we should mention, has hired new management, and we wish them well.) Our after-tax loss from this investment was USD 444 million, about 1/5 of 1% of Berkshire's net worth. In the past 50 years, we have only once realised an investment loss that at the time of sale cost us 2% of our net worth. Twice, we experienced 1% losses. All three of these losses occurred in the 1974-1975 period, when we sold stocks that were very cheap in order to buy others we believed to be even cheaper".

Thus, the incident teaches us that when it is time to sell our stocks i.e., when we know that the investment is not safe, we should not delay or feel afraid of selling the same in the hope of making better profits in future.

Do not vacillate over buying: But Warren Buffett's biggest mistake was a different kind of vacillation. In 2014, he had told the shareholders that almost all his huge errors were in 'not making a purchase' when he should have. In this context, he had mentioned about his serious hesitation in buying Walmart stock. The interesting fact is that Buffett in his annual letter to the shareholders in 1990, had written how low operating costs of Walmart allowed it to sell at prices that its competitors could not touch and it could constantly increase its market share. But Warren Buffett took fifteen years to take a final decision to buy; he had not bought any shares of Walmart before 2005. In the middle of 2016, Buffett was left with Walmart shares worth USD 3 billion, but he started selling the same after that and in February 2017, he had shares worth USD 100 million only. In fact, Buffett had indicated to his shareholders in the very beginning of 2016 that the days of mega retail companies like Walmart were over and future belonged to e-commerce companies like Amazon.

Thus, this serious mistake of Warren Buffett teaches us that we should not vacillate over buying stocks when it is time. Buffett had accepted that had he not hesitated in making investment in Walmart and had he seized the opportunity in 1990 itself and bought Walmart shares then, Berkshire Hathaway's net worth would have gone up by at least USD 50 billion (till 2014). This means that when we know that the future prospects of shares of a particular company is great and we still delay buying the same, it is just like the mistake of not picking a bag of gold lying on a table. Hence, whenever we get a buying opportunity, wc should grab the same.

And...finally, Warren Buffett also advises his managers to keep away from sycophants.

❑